ALL SHALL BE WELL
READINGS FOR LENT AND EASTER

ALL SHALL BE WELL

READINGS FOR
LENT AND EASTER

Michael Leach, James Keane,
Doris Goodnough, editors

ORBIS BOOKS
Maryknoll, New York 10545

ORBIS BOOKS

Founded in 1970, Orbis Books endeavors to publish works that enlighten the mind, nourish the spirit, and challenge the conscience. The publishing arm of the Maryknoll Fathers and Brothers, Orbis seeks to explore the global dimensions of the Christian faith and mission, to invite dialogue with diverse cultures and religious traditions, and to serve the cause of reconciliation and peace. The books published reflect the views of their authors and do not represent the official position of the Maryknoll Society. To learn more about Maryknoll and Orbis Books, please visit our website at www.maryknollsociety.org.

Manufactured in the United States of America.
Design: Roberta Savage

Library of Congress Cataloging-in-Publication Data
All shall be well : readings for Lent and Easter / Michael Leach, James Keane, Doris Goodnough, editors.
   pages cm
  ISBN 978-1-62698-139-3 (pbk.)
   1. Lent—Meditations. 2. Easter—Meditations. I. Leach, Michael, 1940–editor.
BV85.A45 2015
242'.34—dc23   2015023122

❧

"All shall be well, and all shall be well,
and all manner of thing shall be well."

—Julian of Norwich

Because Lent begins on a different date each year in the church calendar, these readings are numbered rather than organized by date, beginning with Ash Wednesday and ending with several selections for Easter.

Contents

All Shall Be Well

Contents

ALL SHALL BE WELL

Contents

ALL SHALL BE WELL

Contents

All Shall Be Well

Contents

ALL SHALL BE WELL

INTRODUCTION

"On that day you will realize that I am in my
Father, and you are in me, and I am in you."

–JOHN 14:20

"And all shall be well."

– JULIAN OF NORWICH

That is Easter, that is the journey of Lent. For 46 days we move beyond the shadow of our egos so the light of Christ that opened a tomb can open our eyes to the astonishing realization that we are *in* him, and thus in God and each other, and all is well.

Easter means no matter how blind we have been we still live in God through Christ Jesus our Lord and are still as God created us (Acts 17:28). This is the atonement, the *at-one-ment* that sets us free. St. Paul said it once and forever:

I am convinced that nothing can ever separate
us from God's love. Not death, not life, angels or
demons, our fears for today or our worries about
tomorrow—not even the powers of hell can separate
us from God's love.

—ROMANS 8:38

This is end of the journey to spiritual wellness that is Lent: for 40 days Jesus fasts and prays and learns and teaches. The devil tempts him. The angels lift him. He cries over Jerusalem. He agonizes in the Garden. He forgives sinners. He suffers, is crucified, and is buried. And then, "on that day," the third day, the day we call Easter, Jesus rises from the dead to save us from sin and convince us that everything he did and said about God and us was true.

For the 46 days between Ash Wednesday and Easter Sunday we too pray and learn: to decrease so that Christ will increase in us (Jn 3:30). We endeavor to lose our false life to gain our real life (Mt 16:25). The season of Lent, the miracle of Easter, is all about waking up from a deep sleep, opening the curtains of unawareness to light, and being alive again. "Awake, O sleeper, and arise from the dead, and Christ will shine on you!" (Eph 5:14).

The stories and images and insights in this book are but candles to light your Lenten path. They begin with words by T.S. Eliot on the journey we begin on Ash Wednesday, and they end with a poem by Gerard Manley Hopkins on Easter's great wonder:

In a flash, at a trumpet crash,

I am all at once what Christ is, since he was what I am, and
  This Jack, joke, poor potsherd, patch, matchwood,
    immortal diamond,
      Is immortal diamond.

In the pages between Paul Raushenbush shares why he *loves* Lent, Ernesto Cardenal guides us through the temptations in the wilderness, Phyllis Tickle celebrates Lent as "the days of greatest calm in the church's year," Henri Nouwen finds Jesus in the outstretched hands of the needy, Julia Alvarez takes us along with Jesus on his way to the cross, Dorothy Day shows us why "love and more love is the only solution," John Updike guarantees us that Jesus' resurrection happened the way the Bible says it did, and 47 other poets, novelists, and essayists break open the spiritual meanings of Lent and Easter with stories, epiphanies, and other surprises.

We hope they will mean something to you, during Lent or Holy Week or any day of the year. Any day is a good day to awaken and be well.

Michael Leach, James Keane, and Doris Goodnough

Ash Wednesday

T. S. Eliot

Blessed sister, holy mother,
    spirit of the fountain, spirit of the garden,
Suffer us not to mock ourselves with falsehood
Teach us to care and not to care
Teach us to sit still
Even among these rocks,
Our peace in His will
And even among these rocks
Sister, mother
And spirit of the river, spirit of the sea,
Suffer me not to be separated

And let my cry come unto Thee.

🌿

Spiritual Medicine

Thomas Merton

Even the darkest moments of the liturgy are filled with joy, and Ash Wednesday, the beginning of the Lenten fast, is a day of happiness, a Christian feast. It cannot be otherwise, as it forms part of the great Easter cycle.

The Paschal Mystery is above all the mystery of life, in which the Church, by celebrating the death and resurrection of Christ, enters into the Kingdom of Life which He has established once for all by His definitive victory over sin and death. We must remember the original meaning of Lent, as the *ver sacrum*, the Church's "holy spring" in which the catechumens were prepared for their baptism, and public penitents were made ready by penance for their restoration to the sacramental life in a communion with the rest of the Church. Lent is then not a season of punishment so much as one of healing. There is joy in the salutary fasting and abstinence of the Christian who eats and drinks less in order that his mind may be more clear and receptive to receive the sacred nourishment of God's word, which the whole Church announces and meditates upon in each day's liturgy throughout Lent. The whole life and teaching of Christ pass before us, and Lent is a season of special reflection and prayer, a forty-day retreat in which each Christian, to the extent that he is able, tries to follow Christ into the desert by prayer and fasting.

Some monks and ascetics will give themselves especially to fasting and vigils, silence and solitude in these days, and they will meditate more deeply on the word of God. But all the faithful should listen to the word as it is announced in the liturgy or in Bible services and respond to it according to their ability. In this way, for the whole Church, Lent will not be merely a season simply of a few formalized penitential practices, half understood and undertaken without interest, but a time of metanoia, the turning of all minds and hearts to God in preparation for the celebration of the Paschal Mystery in which some will for the first time receive the light of Christ; others will be restored to the communion of the faithful, and all will renew their baptismal consecration of their lives to God, in Christ.

The cross of ashes, traced upon the forehead of each Christian, is not only a reminder of death but inevitably (though tacitly) a pledge of resurrection. The ashes of a Christian are no longer mere ashes. The body of a Christian is a temple of the Holy Ghost, and though it is fated to see death, it will return again to life in glory. The cross, with which the ashes are traced upon us, is the sign of Christ's victory over death. The words "Remember, man, that thou art dust, and that to dust thou shalt return" are not to be taken as the quasi-form of a kind of "sacrament of death" (as if such a thing were possible). It might be good stoicism to receive a mere reminder of our condemnation to die, but it is not Christianity. The declaration that the body must fall temporarily into dust is a challenge to spiritual combat, that our burial may be "in Christ" and that we may rise with Him to "live unto God."

The ashes of this Wednesday are not merely a sign of death, but a promise of life to those who do penance. And yet the ashes are clearly a summons to penance, fasting and compunction.

Hence the seemingly paradoxical character of the Ash Wednesday liturgy. The gospel charges us to avoid outward signs of grief and, when we fast, to anoint our heads and to wash our faces. Yet we receive a smear of ashes on our heads. There must be grief in this day of joy. It is a day, we shall see, in which joy and grief go together hand in hand: for that is the meaning of compunction—a sorrow which pierces, which liberates, which gives hope and therefore joy. Compunction is a baptism of sorrow, in which the tears of the penitent are a psychological but also deeply religious purification, preparing and disposing him for the sacramental waters of baptism or for the sacrament of penance. Such sorrow brings joy because it is at once a mature acknowledgment of guilt and the acceptance of its full consequences: hence it implies a religious and moral adjustment to reality, the acceptance of one's actual condition, and the acceptance of reality is always a liberation from the burden of illusion which we strive to justify by our errors and our sins. Compunction is a necessary sorrow, but it is followed by joy and relief because it wins for us one of the greatest blessings: the light of truth and the grace of humility. The tears of the Christian penitent are real tears, but they bring joy.

Only the inner rending, the tearing of the heart, brings this joy. It lets out our sins, and lets in the clean air of God's spring, the sunlight of the days that advance toward Easter. Rending of the garments lets in nothing but the cold. The rending of heart which is spoken of in the lesson from Joel is that "tearing away" from ourselves and our *vetustas*—the "oldness" of the old man, wearied with the boredom and drudgery of an indifferent existence, that we may turn to God and taste His mercy, in the liberty of His sons.

When we turn to Him, what do we find? That "He is gracious and merciful, patient and rich of mercy." He even speaks to us in His own words, saying: "Behold I will send you corn and wine and oil and you shall be filled with them: and I will no more make you a reproach among the nations." This at the beginning of a forty days' fast!

It is necessary that at the beginning of this fast, the Lord should show Himself to us in His mercy. The purpose of Lent is not only expiation, to satisfy the divine justice, but above all a preparation to rejoice in His love. And this preparation consists in receiving the gift of His mercy—a gift which we receive in so far as we open our hearts to it, casting out what cannot remain in the same room with mercy.

Now one of the things we must cast out first of all is fear. Fear narrows the little entrance of our heart. It shrinks up our capacity to love. It freezes up our power to give ourselves. If we were terrified of God as an inexorable judge, we would not confidently await His mercy, or approach Him trustfully in prayer. Our peace, our joy in Lent, are a guarantee of grace.

In laying upon us the light cross of ashes, the Church desires to take off our shoulders all other heavy burdens—the crushing load of worry and obsessive guilt, the dead weight of our own self-love. We should not take upon ourselves a "burden" of penance and stagger into Lent as if we were Atlas, carrying the whole world on his shoulders.

Perhaps there is small likelihood of our doing so. But in any case, penance is conceived by the Church less as a burden than as a liberation. It is only a burden to those who take it up unwillingly. Love makes it light and happy. And that is another reason why Ash Wednesday is filled with the lightness of love.

In some monastic communities, monks go up to receive the ashes barefoot. Going barefoot is a joyous thing. It is good to feel the floor or the earth under your feet. It is good when the whole church is silent, filled with the hush of men walking without shoes. One wonders why we wear such things as shoes anyway. Prayer is so much more meaningful without them. It would be good to take them off in church all the time. But perhaps this might appear quixotic to those who have forgotten such very elementary satisfactions. Someone might catch cold at the mere thought of it—so let's return to the liturgy.

To say there is joy in Ash Wednesday is not to empty the procession of its sorrows and anguish. "Save me O God," we cry at the very beginning, "for the waters are come in even unto my soul." This is not a song of joy. If we present ourselves before God to receive ashes from the hand of the priest it is because we are convinced of our sinfulness.

That is a weak way of putting it. Sin is a thing that needs to be talked about in concrete and existential terms. A sinner, in the way the liturgy understands him, is not a man with a theoretical conviction that violation of the law brings punishment for guilt. A sinner is a drowning man, a sinking ship. The waters are bursting into him on all sides. He is falling apart under the pressure of the storm that has been breaking up his will, and now the waters rush into the hold and he is dragged down. They are closing over his head, and he cries out to God: "the waters are come in even unto my soul."

Ash Wednesday is for people who know what it means for their soul to be logged with these icy waters: all of us are such people, if only we can realize it.

There is confidence everywhere in Ash Wednesday, yet that does not mean unmixed and untroubled security. The confidence of the Christian is always a confidence in spite of darkness and risk, in the presence of peril, with every evidence of possible disaster. "Let us emend for the better in those things in which we have sinned through ignorance: lest suddenly overtaken by the day of death we seek space for repentance and are not able to find it."

The last words are sobering indeed. And note, it is the sins we have not been fully aware of that we must emend. Once again, Lent is not just a time for squaring conscious accounts: but for realizing what we had perhaps not seen before. The light of Lent is given us to help us with this realization.

Nevertheless, the liturgy of Ash Wednesday is not focused on the sinfulness of the penitent but on the mercy of God. The question of sinfulness is raised precisely because this is a day of mercy, and the just do not need a Savior.

Nowhere will we find more tender expressions of the divine mercy than on this day. His mercy is kind. He looks upon us "according to the multitude of Thy tender mercies." In the introit we sing: "Thou hast mercy upon all (*Misereris omnium*), O Lord, and hatest none of the things which Thou hast made, overlooking the sins of men for the sake of repentance and sparing them, because Thou art the Lord our God."

How good are these words of Wisdom in a time when on all sides the Lord is thought by men to be a God who hates. Those who deny Him say they do so because evil in the world could be the work only of a God that hated the world.

But even those who profess to love Him regard Him too often as a furious Father, who seeks only to punish and to revenge Himself for the evil that is done "against Him"—One who cannot abide the slightest contradiction but will immediately mark it down for retribution, and will not let a farthing of the debt go unpaid.

This is not the God, the Father of our Lord Jesus Christ, who Himself "hides" our sins (*dissimulans peccata*) and gets them out of sight, like a mother making quick and efficient repairs on the soiled face of a child just before entering a house where he ought to appear clean. The blessings of the ashes know Him only as the "God who desires not the death of the sinner," "who is moved by humiliation and appeased by satisfaction." He is everywhere shown to us as "plenteous in mercy—*multum misericors.*"

And from the infinite treasure of His mercies He draws forth the gift of compunction. This is a sorrow without servile fear, which is all the more deep and tender as it receives pardon from the tranquil, calm love of the merciful Lord: a love which the Latin liturgy calls, in two untranslatable words, *serenissima pietas.* The God of Ash Wednesday is like a calm sea of mercy. In Him there is no anger.

This "hiding" of God's severity is not a subterfuge. It is a revelation of His true nature. He is not severe, and it is not theologically accurate to say that He becomes angry, that He is moved to hurt and to punish.

He is love. Love becomes severe only to those who make Him severe for themselves. Love is hard only to those who refuse Him. It is not, and cannot be, Love's will to be refused. Therefore it is not and cannot be Love's will to be severe and to punish.

But it is of the very nature of Love that His absence is sorrow and death and punishment. His severity flows not from His own nature but from the fact of our refusal. Those who refuse Him are severe to themselves, and immolate themselves to the blood-thirsty god of their own self-love.

It is from this idol that Love would deliver us. To such bitter servitude, Love would never condemn us.

This brings us to the meaning of the Lenten fast. It is not that food is evil, or that natural satisfactions are something God grudgingly allows us, preferring to deprive us of them when He can.

Fasting is a good thing because food itself is a good thing. But the good things of this world have this about them, that they are good in their season and not out of it. Food is good, but to be constantly eating is a bad thing and in fact it is not even pleasant. The man who gorges himself with food and drink enjoys his surfeiting much less than the fasting person enjoys his frugal collation.

Even the fast itself, in moderation and according to God's will, is a pleasant thing. There are healthy natural joys in self-restraint: joys of the spirit which shares its lightness even with the flesh. Happy is the man whose flesh does not burden his spirit but rests only lightly upon its arm, like a graceful companion.

That is why there is wisdom in fasting. The clear

head and the light step of the one who is not over-fed enable him to see his way and to travel through life with a wiser joy. There is even a profound natural rightness in this fast at the spring of the year.

These reasons are true as far as they go, but they are not in themselves a sufficient explanation of the Lenten fast. Fasting is not merely a natural and ethical discipline for the Christian. It is true that St. Paul evokes the classic comparison of the athlete in training, but the purpose of the Christian fast is not simply to tone up the system, to take off useless fat, and get the body as well as the soul in trim for Easter. The religious meaning of the Lenten fast is deeper than that. Our fasting is to be seen in the context of life and death, and St. Paul made clear that he brought his body into subjection not merely for the good of the soul, but that the whole man might not be "cast away." In other words the Christian fast is something essentially different from a philosophical and ethical discipline for the good of the mind. It has a part in the work of salvation, and therefore in the Paschal mystery. The Christian must deny himself, whether by fasting or in some other way, in order to make clear his participation, and therefore in the Paschal mystery. The mystery of our burial with Christ in order to rise with Him to a new life. This cannot be merely a matter of "interior acts" and "good intentions." It is not supposed to be something purely "mental" and subjective. That is why fasting is proposed to the Christian by long tradition and by the Bible itself as a concrete way of expressing one's self-denial in imitation of Christ and in participation with His mysteries.

It is true that the present discipline of the Church, for serious reasons, has alleviated the obligation of fasting and in some areas has done away with it altogether. But certainly the Christian should desire, if he is able, to participate in this ancient Lenten observance which is so necessary for a genuine understanding of the meaning of the Paschal Mystery.

Finally, the ashes themselves are spiritual medicine, like all the sacramentals. The fruits of these apparently sterile ashes are wonderfully rich! Great is the secret power imparted to them by the influence of the risen body of Christ, who by His victory has become "life-giving Spirit."

The riches of this sacramental are clear from the prayers of the blessing. Blessed and sanctified by the sign of the cross, the ashes become a "*remedium salubre*" (health-giving medicine) and they bring *sanitas* (wholeness, cleanness) to the body as well as protection to the soul (*animae tutelam*), both of these availing for the remission of sins. They bring the grace of that humility which they signify, they bring also the pardon which we implore by the fact of receiving them.

They bring at the same time a realization of the horror of sin, and confidence of forgiveness. They bring with them all the aids necessary for the holy war of Lent, and they impart a special efficacy to our Lenten penances and prayers.

In a word, the ashes sign our whole being with the merciful blessing of God.

Armed with the grace of this great sacramental we begin a four-day preparation for Lent. For, as some may be surprised to learn, Ash Wednesday is not the beginning of Lent, but only the beginning of the Lenten Fast.

The liturgical time of Lent begins on the following Sunday, and here the liturgy has a different character. It is more ancient and therefore more objective. The structure of the Sunday Mass is loftier and more noble in its splendidly simple architecture. Nothing is said about how a sinner feels, and the question of any possible conflict between the mercy and justice of God is not raised. All is bathed in the same pure light, the light of the wilderness where Christ the Lord fasts in solitude and is tempted by the devil.

The dramatic, medieval rites of Ash Wednesday may perhaps make a stronger and more immediate appeal to our feelings. The Mass of the first Sunday however leads us deeper into the real mystery of Lent, uniting us more profoundly and more directly with the Christ who, praying and fasting in us, will purify us and offer us together with Himself to the Father in the glory of His Easter victory.

3

ৎ~

A Time to Heal

Joan Chittister, OSB

I remember the rush of insight that seeped through me the day I realized the situation. It had suddenly occurred to me that none of us can really be sure that we understand the Book of Ecclesiastes. What's more, I realized that maybe no one is supposed to be able to grasp its meanings completely, in one burst of consciousness, in one gift of light. Maybe it is supposed to come over us slowly, in layers, one bright moment at a time when life becomes new with pain, fresh with joy, different from its beginnings. Maybe it is the very obscurity of the Book of Ecclesiastes that is its meaning.

The problem with the book lies in the fact that it is very deceptive. It reads with such simplicity that, at first glance, it stands there disarmingly transparent, almost simplistic—"a time for this, a time for that," it insists—monotonous and droning, hypnotic and obvious, and, apparently, of not much use. Unless, of course, you think a little. For instance, I realized as I began to struggle with the themes in it that what was actually being said by the statement about "a time to heal" was not one message but two. At the first level, its clear sense is not only that there is a time in every life for a person to care about the sufferings of other people, but that there is some obligation to abate them. On the other hand, it is equally clear that the dictum could also mean that there's a period of time in every human life when the process of being healed, of coming beyond my own woundedness, may itself be life's greatest project.

Isn't the implication, then, that personal healing, the cauterization of personal wounds, is part of the natural rhythm of life? That we all need it on every level? That we must all go through it someday or run the risk, ironically, of never being whole because we have never known what it is to be wounded but then healed, to be struck down but still survive? Suffering, after all, is surely not for its own sake.

The thought becomes a haunting challenge. What

is it to be beaten by life to the point of death? What is really the role of the good Samaritans of the world? Most of all, how do we come to healing once we've been battered beyond any energy for it? And, finally, who of those figures am I myself at this point in my life—the healer or the one in need of healing? And if I am the one in need of healing, what is my own role in it?

"Calamity is the human's true touchstone," Beaumont wrote. Calamity, in other words, lets loose the fire that tries the gold, the wind that tests the tree, the water that sweeps away everything in life that is not anchored, not grounded, not imbedded in the firmament of our souls. Without calamity what shall we ever be and how shall we ever know it? "I survived the San Francisco earthquake," the T-shirts said. What I had once regarded as a cruel joke, I began to see as a statement of theology, a fierce proclamation of the spirit, rather than the flip response of a culture so unaccustomed to disaster that mockery substitutes for respect. There is, indeed, a time to heal, important to the healthy, essential to the strong, waiting its moment in each of us.

Healing eludes us, however, at every level of the personal and the political spectrum. People die and leave us aching. Old hurts still sear. Around us, like ghosts stalking in the night, our world erupts in tiny sores of violence and brutality while we watch helpless on television screens in every pub and waiting room in the land. Inside ourselves we feel the pain; outside ourselves we wear a calloused look. We have learned to yawn our way through suffering in volumes unimaginable to generations before us. Healing has become the art of political deals and military violence masking as righteousness on the public level or showing as anger and distance on the personal level. What we cannot resolve we repress. What we cannot control we constrain. But we do not heal. Too often, the pain remains embedded in the human psyche, raw and inflamed, waiting only to vent itself again. We build our defenses, personal and public, higher and higher, always on the ready for the next chance to attack, to take vengeance on those who were vengeful toward us, to hurt what we cannot control. Indeed we do not heal; we simply contain the diseases of the soul under thin veneers of pious virtue as we lie in wait.

One of the most health-conscious cultures on earth, we spend huge sums of money on physical well-being all the time being battered in soul. In a society driven by immensely unhealthy motives of achievement and power, profit and personal acceptance, we find ourselves so bent on winning we are surely doomed to fail. We run faster every day and accomplish less despite it. Worse, perhaps, when we have ground ourselves to the psychological pulp that follows competition and precedes loneliness or rejection or the isolating consequences of success, we sit down in the midst of the pain around us and quit. We lose friends and lose energy and lose hope. We lose the family or the race or the security we had taken for granted. We find in its place a cold, stiff copy of the life we once knew, full of hurt and rupture, tormented by an acrid soul and a bruised heart. The work fails, the relationship ends, the future clouds, the sand shifts. We come to the point where we would rather die inside than try again to reshape what would not bend.

The question is, why? Why do we hold pain to the breast like a fox under a toga that eats our insides out even as we smile? "I'm fine," we say when we do not mean it. "Nothing's wrong," we say when we seethe with hurt. "That's life," we snap when life has struck so hard we would prefer no life at all. "Just ignore it," we say when hurt drives out joy, stampedes trust, consumes our hearts, and saps our every thought.

Then, because we have not attended to the wounds in ourselves, we have no capacity for the pain of others. Because we ourselves have too often refused to heal, we cannot heal others. It is a fearsome carousel, this anesthetizing of the human soul. It jades and blocks and makes us paranoid. It cools us and distances us and leaves us hard of heart. Those who swallow stones, we learn, become stones.

Indeed there is "a time to heal." But how? Healing depends on our own resolve to go out of our way to do what we would not, in any circumstances, choose to do. Healing requires that we reach out, not necessarily to those who have hurt us, but at least to something that gives us new life, new hope, new pleasure. Healing is the process of refusing to be wounded.

The parable of the good Samaritan is not about the curing of one person; it is about the healing of two, both of whom carry the scars of abuse, both of whom reside in us in tandem at all times. One has been beaten in body; the other in soul. One has been wounded by the brutality of people; the other has been wounded by ideas that cripple and limit, that bind a person to small, small worlds and smother the air we breathe. The Samaritan, the outcast, has been wounded and overlooked by society. The Levite, the professional religious of the Establishment culture, has been taught to ignore the wounds of those who do not meet with public approval and so, made close-minded and socially limited, is wounded too. One posture teaches us fear; the other perspective teaches us hate. Whatever the situation, the end result is pain. The question is, how shall either of the battered learn to live again?

Who has not known what it is to be hurt by either hate or neglect, to be passed by on the road of life by those from whom we thought we could certainly expect help? Who has not known what it is to be targeted for scorn or rejection or jealousy or misinterpretation? Who has not felt the stultifying effects of ideas that make us captive to the agendas and ambitions of others and leave us as much oppressed as oppressor? What is the process, then, of coming to wholeness again, once the bonds of human community have been broken? What repairs the breaking of a golden cord? You see, the fact is that enemies can damage us, but they cannot hurt us. Only people we love can do that by what they withhold from us that could give us life, by the lies they teach us that nail our feet to the ground.

There are two obstacles to being healed. The first

lies in our attachment to the pain. We cannot heal ourselves of the pains to which we cling. We have to want to be healed. We cannot wear injustice like a red badge of courage and hope to rise from it. Even before we are vindicated, even before restitution comes—if it ever comes—we ourselves must move beyond it, outside of it, despite it.

Healing depends on our wanting to be well. I may not forget the blows I have suffered in life, but I must not choose to live under their power forever. Most of all, I must not choose to imprison myself in my own pain. Whatever has mutilated us—the betrayal, the dishonesty, the mockery, the broken promises—there is more to life than that. The first step of healing, then, is to find new joy for myself to tide me through the terror of the abandonment. It is time to get a life instead of mourning one. When the beating is over, there is nothing to do but to get up and go on, in a different direction to be sure, but on, definitely on.

The second step in healing is to find new ideas in which to live. Whatever we needed before the breakpoint came—security, love, connectedness, certainty, identity—we must now find someplace else. We must put our hope in risk and find it challenging, in self and find it strong, in newness and find it enough.

The third step to healing is to trust ourselves to someone else just when we think we cannot trust anyone or anything at all. Just when we are not sure who the enemy really is, we must risk confidence in someone again. It is a false and hollow cure that ends with a sterile handshake. Healing comes for both the beaten and the intellectually bound when they step across the lines in their minds and hope that this time, in this person, in this situation, they will find the acceptance, the enlightenment, needed to join the human community one more time.

Healing comes when I have been able to desensitize myself to the indignity of hurt by telling it to death until I have bored even myself with the story. For this I need the Samaritans, the healers, who by taking me into the arms of the heart to let me cry transcend their own small lives and learn about the human condition what they themselves would never have come to, perhaps, without me. We need the Samaritan who listens and understands. It is not the wounding that kills; it is lack of understanding that paralyzes the soul. It is, after all, understanding that every soul on earth is seeking.

The final step in healing is a matter of time itself. To honor the fact that there is "a time for healing" means surely that we come to peace with the notion that healing does not come before its time, that healing takes time, that time itself is a healer who comes slowly, bringing new life and new wisdom in its wake.

The spiritual advantages of healing are obvious for the healer. Healers come to new levels of compassion. Once able to be important in someone else's life, healers come to a new sense of their own personal value. Those who bind the emotional wounds of others find new meaning in life and new love for the unknown other. Those who touch the bleeding soul of another to shape it into new confidence and fresh hope are themselves flooded with a sense of compassionate power. The spiritual advantages of the healing process in healers too are often overlooked. We assume that healing is gratuitous condescension rather than a spiritual discipline of immense proportion and great reward.

Most of all, however, it is the spiritual power of the healing process in each of us that goes unnoted and so unappreciated. We flee the hurts—ignore them and dismiss them and detest them—and so miss the values of the healing time itself. "Where there is sorrow, there is holy ground," Wilde teaches. It is in the healing process that we come to a new appreciation of life.

What the human being survives is the mark of the mettle of humanity. What we manage to transcend is what we have triumphed over. What we have wrestled with and won is what measures in us the quality of our lives.

The Samaritan, by reaching out and touching the pain of another, throws her own life open to new significance. The wounded who walk away from their pain into unknown and unsought ways instead of spending life awash in it show all of us that life upon life awaits those whose minds are made up to live, whatever the beatings, whatever the traps, whatever the muggings along the way. "Pain is life," Charles Lamb wrote. "The sharper the pain, the more evidence of life." Pain, we learn as life goes on, is simply one more entrance into life, one more challenge to change things.

🖋

4

Why I Love Lent

Paul Brandeis Raushenbush

I wasn't raised in a household that observed Lent and only began to get into it once I was introduced to the more liturgical traditions while at seminary. My mother always thought it odd that I would observe this season, believing that one of the finer things about being a Protestant was not having to do dreary old Lent.

However, Lent has become my favorite season and Ash Wednesday my favorite Christian holy day outside of Holy Week. Having someone look you in the eye with love and tell you that you are going to die is powerfully moving and quite beautiful, especially, I suppose, if that day doesn't seem too close.

"Death is the mother of beauty. Only the perishable can be beautiful, which is why we are unmoved by artificial flowers," said Wallace Stevens.

Being reminded that I am perishable, that I am dust, and that I will return to dust serves to awaken me to the fact that I am on that beautiful journey between dust to dust that we call life. I, like those dry bones in Ezekiel, have had life-breath breathed into me. Ash Wednesday and the season of Lent startle me enough to consider that this very day might be a good day to look up from my day to day concerns, as unimportant as they may be, and to zoom out the lens and to look at my life—where I have been, where I am going, and if all is well with my soul right here and now.

In Lent we observe the forty days that Jesus wandered in the wilderness filled with trial and temptation. As it is with most of us, my personal sojourn often is located in the wilderness; winding within uncomfortable and uncertain terrain filled with temptations and trials and sense of alone-ness. At some point in my life, however, I came across the words of another sojourner found in Psalm 139: "Where can I go from your spirit? Or where can I flee from your presence?" the psalmist writes. "If I ascend to heaven, you are there; if I make my bed in Sheol, you are there. If I take the wings of the morning and settle at the farthest limits of the sea, even there your hand shall lead me, and your right hand shall hold me fast. If I say, 'Surely the darkness shall cover me, and the light around me become night,' even the darkness is not dark to you; the night is as bright as the day, for darkness is as light to you."

Over time, the testimony of God's intimate presence and love found in this psalm has become my own, and, while it did not, and has not relieved me of my wilderness experiences it allows me to understand my struggles in a different way, to feel less alone and to redeem my life as a valid and, even valued, part of the wider sacred story of God.

Maybe that is why I love Lent. In this season it is permitted to reflect on the pain in our lives and to even acknowledge that there are times when God seems utterly absent. Christians spend their lives between the words of Jesus that ask God, why have you forsaken me, and the others that proclaim into your hands I commend my spirit. The testimony of Psalm 139 is that no matter where we go, or what we do, whether we sense God, or we don't—God is. God is Present.

Lent offers us the opportunity to tear away all that would blind us, or numb us to that reality. For some that will come through fasting from mindless consumption of whatever distracts us; for others it will come from radical service to the neighbor; but what is most important about Lent is that we make time and space for an awareness that God who is with us and loves us—even right here and now. It is in the telling of our stories that God is revealed, and Jesus, the cross, and the resurrection become real—all of our lives become the bread and the cup—elements of eternal life amidst the dust.

5

Why I'm Committed to Lent

Mallory McDuff

In Fairhope, Alabama, I grew up in a family of six where giving up something for Lent was an expectation, not a choice. A few days before Ash Wednesday, the dinner conversation revolved around one question: "What you are giving up for Lent?"

As children, we sacrificed the usual suspects of chocolate, chips, ice cream, and TV. When my brother Laurence gave up TV one year, he walked backwards through the living room with his hands over his ears to avoid confronting the television screen with its Saturday night lineup of *Love Boat* and *Fantasy Island.*

My parents gave up indulgences like alcohol and meat, and then several years later, they became teetotalers and vegetarians. "I just feel better without a headache after a party," explained my mother when I challenged her abstinence from alcohol, a practice that eluded my understanding as a college student. For my parents, Lent became a way to experiment with simpler living and then integrate those practices into their lives.

One year, we gave up trash for Lent, long before the advent of recycling programs or warehouse stores like Sam's Club. My mother bought items in bulk, like flour, rice, and sugar, from a mail-order catalog and found eggs from a local farmer. I remember burning cardboard packaging in the wood stove and composting food wastes in the backyard. But I was too self-absorbed as a teenager to feel any negative impact of giving up trash or to consider the intersection of our Lenten practice with the world around me.

• • •

Now as the parent of ninth- and second-grade daughters, I am the only family member committed to self-denial for the forty-six days of Lent, which includes forty days plus six Sundays. Last year, when I gave up alcohol for Lent, I replaced my nightly ritual of having one or two beers with the practice of drinking herbal tea, one cup after another, from dinner until bedtime. This year, I am giving up both alcohol and Facebook, two consumptive activities that offer escape and entertainment.

Just last week, I ate supper with my eight-year-old Annie Sky at a local pub called Wicked Weed that specializes in high-gravity hoppy beers. After a challenging week with my teenager, I considered breaking my fast—just this once—and ordering an IPA with my black bean burger with pimento cheese. I felt like I deserved this treat, especially after watching other customers with their pint glasses on the patio in the warm afternoon sun. (Clearly, my initial mistake was letting my daughter pick the restaurant.)

As I glanced at the beer menu, Annie Sky looked appalled. "You are NOT going to break Lent!" she said. "It's like saying you are doing something but not doing it! What would be the point?" A bit embarrassed, I put down the menu and ordered a glass of water with lemon.

After a month of drinking herbal teas this Lent, I have memorized the inspirational sayings stapled to each Yogi tea bag: "The purpose of life is to enjoy every moment." "Mental happiness is total relaxation." "Act, don't react." These pithy sayings actually fuel my own reflection about why I am so committed to Lent:

As a Christian, I give up something for Lent because Jesus went into the wilderness to fast for forty days. I yearn to be a part of something larger than myself, to sacrifice something small, recognizing that our world needs less consumption and more contemplation.

As a mother, I give up something for Lent because I want my daughters to know that I can survive six weeks without drinking a beer after work. And I want to remind myself that I can.

As a teacher, I give up something for Lent because I am weary of the dopamine hits from checking e-mail and Facebook and the headlines, as if I am checking the pulse of patient. For six weeks, I need to practice a pause.

As a child of God, I give up something for Lent because I have experienced losses: a mother, a father, an unborn child, a marriage.

As a person of hope, I give up something for Lent because I want to prepare for a celebration.

• • •

Certainly doubters will question the rationale of sacrificing small indulgences for one season in the liturgical calendar. In fact, the blog "Think Christian" outlines several humorous reasons not to give up something for Lent, which include:

"It's not the self-denial Olympics."

"Chocolate ain't a cross."

"We're not trying to beat Christ at his own game."

Despite these legitimate protests, Lenten practices continue, morphing with our social mores such as taking "selfies" after Ash Wednesday services and announcing the self-denial of Twitter with a tweet. In fact, Stephen Smith, who runs LentTracker for BibleGateway.com, publishes an index meter with the most mentioned Lenten topics on Twitter. The top ten sacrifices this year included chocolate, Twitter, swearing, alcohol, soda, and social networking, among others.

But my enduring loyalty to Lent reflects my parents, who allowed spiritual discipline to spill into their daily lives, as they consumed fewer resources with every additional year that they lived. Giving up trash one year and even driving the next, my father actually could have won the self-denial Olympics, if the U.S. were recruiting outside the demographic of monks and nuns.

But for him, Lent was about living better, not worse.

Unlike my parents, I probably won't give up alcohol and Facebook forever, at least not yet. But I honor this practice each year, because it is a way to honor them. In truth, I am addicted to their love, and almost a decade after their sudden and untimely deaths, I still don't know how I am living without them. I am confounded that I can raise children without their advice. I want a hit of their love every morning when I wake underneath my mother's quilt and every night when I nestle my cheek into my youngest daughter's neck, whose heat melts my own urgency to get her into bed and asleep.

Ageless metaphors like life as a journey and the unknown as a wilderness may seem like cheap wisdom attached to organic tea bags. But life is like a forced Lent, where we don't get to choose the things we have to give up. Choosing to give something up is a means of acknowledging and redeeming what is lost. In this practice, we draw closer to a life that is not giving up—on love.

🖎

6

Bothering to Love: One Priest's Modest Proposal for Lent

James Martin, SJ

What have you given up for Lent?

That's what many Christians—from almost every denomination, and especially Roman Catholics—are asking one another this time of year. The most common thing to forego, I would wager, is some kind of food: soda and chocolate seem to be the Most Favored Sacrifices, with cigarettes and liquor running a close third. Each year, in fact, a Jewish friend from my college days calls me on Ash Wednesday to tell me what to give up, since he thinks my deciding on my own is too easy. Last year it was chicken wings, which was harder than you might think. (I'll save the story of how he came to assign my abstinence for another time.)

Fasting originated as a way of saving money on food, so that Christians could give it to the poor. It had a practical end: no meat for you meant more money for those who couldn't afford meat. Giving things up also reminds you that you don't always have to give into your appetites. It reminds you of your ability to exert self-control. And it reminds you of the poor, who go without every day, Lent or not. The Dutch spiritual writer and Catholic priest Henri Nouwen summed it up nicely: "For now, it seems that some fasting is the best way to remind myself of the millions who are hungry and to purify my heart and mind for a decision that does not exclude them."

Some people see Lenten sacrifices as another example of religious masochism. But look at it this way: People diet for physical reasons, so why not for spiritual ones? If you spend hours in the gym for a great body why not do something healthy to free your spirit from what St. Ignatius Loyola, the 16th-century founder of the Jesuit Order, called "disordered affections." Often Christians abstain from unhealthy things they've been unsuccessfully trying to avoid all year—like junk food or too much TV.

But this Lent I'd like to suggest not giving something up, but doing something.

Specifically, bothering.

In the Gospels, when Jesus of Nazareth condemns people, or points out sin, it's usually not people who are trying hard to avod sinning, it's people who aren't bothering to love. In the famous parable of the Good Samaritan, in the Gospel of Luke, two men pass by a guy lying by the side of the road, who could certainly use some help. They could help the fellow, but they don't. He rightly points out their sin. Jesus doesn't condemn those who are weak and trying hard; but those who are strong and aren't trying at all.

For Jesus, sin is often a failure to bother to love, what theologians used to call a "sin of omission."

But during the weeks before Easter, most Christians seem stuck on what they've been trying to avoid for years. A familiar hymn is: "I try to stop smoking every time Ash Wednesday comes around!" But if Jesus were around today (I know that's a dicey few words) he might say, "Don't worry about where you're already trying and keep failing. Look at where you're not even bothering."

So this Lent, instead of fasting, why not bother? Instead of a negative Lent, how about a positive one?

Instead of giving up chocolate for the umpteenth year in a row, or trying to kick your smoking habit, why not bother to call a friend who's lonely? Instead of turning off your TV, or going to the gym, bother to donate money to the poor in Haiti. Instead of passing up potato chips, bother to visit a sick relative.

In the Gospels Jesus says, "It is mercy I desire, not sacrifice." Here's a novel idea for Lent: why not take Jesus at his word?

7

Lenten Observance Transforms Us from Cacophony to Symphony

Christopher Frechette

Lent is upon us. How does it grab your imagination? By now you've likely decided what to give up this year, how to donate alms, when to give prayer some extra time . . . all of these may have been on your mind, but where has your imagination gone? For several years now, mine has been returning to an image that helps both my personal prayer and my participation in liturgy. It also grounds my reflections on almsgiving and fasting.

Imagine attending a symphony or school orchestra concert. Picture arriving with the crowd and anticipating how you will relax and enjoy the music. Behind the sounds of chatter and movement, hear the instruments as they warm up. Dozens of different instruments are playing in complete disregard for each other, some engaged in sweeping scales, others going over this or that bit of melody. The sounds simply clash—quite literally a cacophony. I actually enjoy this, but I wouldn't be there if the orchestra was intent on doing nothing else all evening.

At a certain moment all the instruments go quiet, which cues the crowd to quiet down, too. Into that silence, an oboist sounds one clear note, an A. Then, all the other instruments match that note, resonating in a unison made striking by contrast to the cacophony that it replaces. Tuning to one instrument helps to ensure that all the instruments will harmonize well with each other in the music they are about to produce.

Just as tuning to the oboe allows the instruments to resonate well with each other, so Lent offers the church community a season to tend to the way in which we resonate together in Christ. This image helps me to take in the seemingly paradoxical power of Lent, one that can draw us as church into union precisely by revealing to us those things that can easily drive us apart. Lent is not primarily about what we do as individuals. It is about helping us to face the reality of ourselves honestly and in tune with the healing presence of Christ in the midst of whatever pain or shame we may feel, and it's about doing all this in solidarity with each other.

What often prevents us from addressing the cacophony in our hearts is pain, whether the pain of knowing we have caused injury or the pain of the injuries done to us that may underlie our own problematic attitudes and behaviors. Such pain may prevent us from looking deeper into its root causes. We may slip into denial and even attempt to run away from the deeper reality behind what we do to hurt ourselves and others. Since such pain can run deep, we may need to face it gradually, and Lent provides us an entire season to focus on it.

Moreover, when confronted by our mistakes, we may feel a kind of shame that can lead to a sense of isolation from one another. Lent confronts us with the reality of our internal noise but not in order to humiliate us or isolate us. Lenten observance transforms acknowledgement of the mystery of sin from a source of isolation to a point of solidarity. Lent is the church's bold invitation to face reality and to draw support from Christ's compassionate and healing presence in our midst. The resulting dynamic is similar to that of meetings in the twelve-step tradition of recovery from addictions. In those meetings, participants acknowledge their common struggle and resolve to rely on their higher power for help. For these participants as well as for the church during Lent, such shared honesty and commitment to grace provide a communal matrix for healing transformation.

Throughout Lent, the church invites us as community to intensify our efforts to listen honestly to our own hearts and to the needs of those around us. We quiet down our attempts to distract ourselves from the difficult realities inside us, much like the instruments of the orchestra stop their cacophony in order to hear the oboe. The goal is not to leave us depressed about the problems in our lives or in our world, but to help us hear Christ's compassionate and healing presence seeking to resonate in both. As Christ's peace grows within us, our ability to attend generously to the needs of others also grows. Our Lenten observance allows us to hear the single note that is Christ's presence transforming us into a community whose lives can proclaim the joy of the Resurrection with the power and beauty of a symphony.

$\sim$

Under the Great Rock

Carlo Carretto

The track, white in the sun, wound ahead of me in a vague outline. The furrows in the sand made by the wheels of the great oil trucks forced me to keep alert every second, if I was to keep the jeep on the move.

The sun was high in the sky, and I felt tired. Only the wind blowing on the hood of the car allowed the jeep to continue, although the temperature was like hell-fire and the water was boiling in the radiator. Every now and then I fixed my gaze on the horizon. I knew that in the area there were great blocks of granite embedded in the sand: they provided highly desirable sources of shade under which to pitch camp and wait the evening before proceeding with the journey.

In fact, towards mid-day, I found what I was looking for. Great rocks appeared on the left of the track. I approached, in the hope that I would find a little shade. I was not disappointed. On the north wall of the thirty foot high slab of stone, a knife of shade was thrown onto the red sand. I pulled the jeep against the wind to cool the engine and unloaded the *ghess*, the necessary equipment for pitching camp: a bag of food, two blankets, and a tripod for the fire.

But approaching the rock I realized that in the shade there were some guests already there: two snakes were curled up in the warm sand, watching me motionlessly. I leapt backwards and retreated to the jeep without taking my eyes off the two serpents. I took the gun, an old contraption lent me by a native who used it to get rid of the jackals which, urged on by hunger and thirst, used to attack his flocks.

I loaded the gun, drew back a bit and took aim in order to try to hit the two snakes together, so as not to waste another bullet.

I fired, and saw the two beasts leap into the air in a cloud of sand. When I was cleaning up the blood and the remains of the snakes I saw, coming out of the mangled entrails of one of them, a bird he hadn't had time to digest. I spread out the mat. In the desert it is everything: chapel, dining-room, bedroom, draw-ing-room. It was the hour of Sext. I sat down, took out my breviary, and recited a few Psalms, but I had to force myself because I was so tired. Besides, every now and then the wind blew fragments of the two vipers I had killed onto the verses I was reading. Warm sultry air was coming from the south and my head ached. I got up. I calculated how much water I had to last me until I reached the well of Tit, and decided to sacrifice a little. From the goatskin gourd I drew a basinful of two pints and poured it on my head. The water soaked into my turban, ran down my neck and on to my clothes. The wind did the rest. From 115° the temperature descended in a few minutes to 80°. With that sense of refreshment I stretched out on the sand to sleep; in the desert you take your siesta before your meal.

In order to lie more comfortably I looked for a blanket to put under my head. I had two. One remained by my side unused, and as I looked at it I could not feel at ease.

But to understand you must hear my story.

The evening before I had passed through Irafog, a small village of Negroes, ex-slaves of the Tuareg. As usual when one reaches a village the people ran out to crowd round the jeep, either from curiosity, or to obtain the various things which desert-travelers bring with them: they may bring a little tea, distribute medicines, or hand over letters.

That evening I had seen old Kada trembling with cold. It seems strange to speak of cold in the desert, but it is so; in fact the Sahara is often called "a cold country where it is very hot in the sun." The sun had gone down, and Kada was shivering. I had the idea of giving him one of the blankets I had with me, an essential part of my *ghess*; but I put the thought out of my mind. I thought of the night and I knew that I, too, would shiver. The little charity that was in me made me think again, though reasoning that my skin wasn't worth more than his and that I had best give him one of the blankets. Even if I shivered a little that was the least a Little Brother could do.

When I left the village the blankets were still on the jeep; and now they were giving me a bad conscience.

I tried to get to sleep with my feet resting on the great rock, but I couldn't manage it. I remembered that a month ago a Tuareg in the middle of his siesta had been crushed by a falling slab. I got up to make sure how stable the boulder was; I saw that it was a little off balance, but not enough to be dangerous.

I lay down again on the sand. If I were to tell you what I dreamed of you would find it strange. The funny thing is that I dreamed that I was asleep under the great boulder and that at a given moment—it didn't seem to be a dream at all: I saw the rock moving, and I felt the boulder fall on top of me. What a nightmare! I felt my bones grating and I found myself dead. No, alive, but with my body crushed under the stone. I was amazed that not a bone hurt; but I could not move. I opened my eyes and saw Kada shivering in front of me at Irafog. I didn't hesitate for a minute to give him the blanket, especially as it was lying unused behind me, a yard away. I tried to stretch out my hand to offer it to him; but the stone made even the smallest movement impossible. I understood what purgatory was and that the suffering of the soul was "no longer to have the possibility of doing what before one could and should have done." Who knows for how many years afterwards I would be haunted by seeing that blanket near me as a witness to my selfishness and to the fact that I was too immature to enter the Kingdom of Love.

I tried to think of how long I was to remain under the rock. The reply was given me by the catechism: "Until you are capable of an act of perfect love." At that moment I felt quite incapable.

The perfect act of love is Jesus going up to Calvary to die for us all. As a member of his Mystical Body I was being asked to show if I was close enough to that perfect love to follow my master to Calvary for the salvation of my brethren. The presence of the blanket denied to Kada the evening before told me that I had still a long way to go. If I were capable of passing by a brother who was shivering with cold, how should I be capable of dying for him in imitation of Jesus who died for us all? In this way I understood that I was lost, and that if somebody had not come to my aid, I should have lain there, aeon after aeon, without being able to move.

I looked away and realized that all those great rocks in the desert were nothing more than the tombs of other men. They too, judged according to their ability to love and found cold, were there to await him who once said, "I shall raise you up on the last day."

❧

9

I Hope You Find

Ita Ford, MM

Dear Jennifer,

The odds that this note will arrive for your birthday are poor, but know I'm with you in spirit as you celebrate sixteen big ones. I hope it's a special day for you.

I want to say something to you and wish I were there to talk to you, because sometimes letters don't get across all the meaning and feeling. But I'll give it a try anyway.

First of all, I love you and care about you and how you are. I'm sure you know that, and that holds if you're an angel or a "goof-off," a genius or a jerk. A lot of that is up to you and what you decide to do with your life.

What I want to say—some of it isn't too jolly birthday talk, but it's real.

Yesterday, I stood looking down at a sixteen-year-old boy who had been killed a few hours earlier. I know a lot of kids even younger who are dead. This is a terrible time in El Salvador for youth. A lot of idealism and commitment is getting snuffed out here now.

The reasons why so many people are being killed are quite complicated, yet there are some clear simple strands. One is that many people have found a meaning to life, to sacrifice, to struggle and even to death! And whether their life spans sixteen years or sixty or ninety, for them their life has had a purpose. In many ways, they are fortunate people. Brooklyn is not passing through the drama of El Salvador, but some things hold true wherever one is and at whatever age. What I am saying is I hope you come to find that which gives life a deep meaning for you. Something worth living for, maybe even worth dying for, something that energizes you, enthuses you, enables you to keep moving ahead.

I can't tell you what it might be. That's for you to find, to choose, to love. I just encourage you to start looking and support you in the search.

Maybe this sounds weird and off the wall and,

maybe, no one else will talk to you like this, but then, too, I'm seeing and living things that others around you aren't. I also gather that you haven't been straining yourself this year in school. Maybe you're into a drifting phase. I don't know. You or no one else has said. All I know is that I want to say to you: Don't waste the gifts and opportunities you have to make yourself and other people happy. Do yourself and a lot of others a favor and get moving again.

I hope this doesn't sound like some kind of a sermon. In fact, it's my birthday present to you. If it doesn't make sense right at this moment, keep this and read it some time from now. Maybe it will be clearer. Or ask me about it, okay?

A very happy birthday to you and much,

Much love!

Ita

≈

10

A God Who Provides

Rob Bell

"Take your only son, whom you love, and sacrifice him there. . . ."

This passage is a classic example of the kind of story that you find in the Bible which causes many people to ask, *"What does a story like this, about a man named Abraham and his son, possibly have to teach us?"* And to be more specific, *"What kind of God would ask a man to sacrifice his son?"*

That's the question, isn't it? The answer is found by looking into a brief history of religion, and bringing to light some details of the story.

Early humans came to the realization that their survival as a species was dependent upon things like food and water. In order for food to grow, it needs sunlight and water in proper proportions. Too much water and things wash away, but not enough and plants die. Too much sunlight and plants wilt, yet not enough and they die. These basic observations brought people to the conclusion that they were dependent upon *unseen forces for their survival, and for which they had no control.* This was actually a monumental leap for that time!

The belief (I use that word intentionally) arose that these *forces* are either on your side, or not. But how do you keep these forces on your side? The next time you have a harvest, you take a portion of that harvest and you offer it on an altar as a sign of your gratitude. Because you need the forces (gods and goddesses) on your side. Now imagine what happened when people would offer a sacrifice, but then it didn't rain, or the sun didn't shine, or their animals still got diseases, or they were unable to have children. Obviously, they concluded that they hadn't offered enough! And so they offered more and more and more. *Anxiety* was built into this form of religion from the beginning. One never knew where you stood with the gods. The thought became that the gods are angry, demanding, and if you don't please them they will punish you by bringing calamity.

But what if things went well? What if it rained just the right amount and the sun shined just the right amount—what if it appeared that the gods were pleased with you? Well then, you'd need to offer them thanks. But how would you ever know if you'd properly showed them how grateful you were? How would you know you'd offered enough? If things went well, you never knew if you'd been grateful enough or offered enough. But if things didn't go well, then clearly you hadn't done . . . enough. Either way, there was *anxiety*.

Now, stay with me here, because this is where things get dodgy: Whether things went well or not, the answer was always *sacrifice more. Give more. Offer more.* This was because you never knew where you stood with the gods. And so you'd offer part of your crop. Then you'd offer a goat and maybe a lamb, a cow, a few cows, or even some birds! The very nature of early religion is that everything escalated because in your anxiety to please the gods you kept having to offer more. What's the most valuable thing you could offer the gods to show them how serious you were about earning their favor? A child, of course. Can you see how child sacrifice lurks on the edges of the Old Testament? It's where religion took you to the place where you'd offer that which was most valuable to you.

Now, on to the Abraham story.

When God tells Abraham to offer his son, he isn't shocked, because, *"early the next morning Abraham got up and loaded his donkey."*

Abraham gets right to it. He doesn't argue, he doesn't protest, he doesn't drag his feet. He clearly knows what to do, and so he does it, of course. That's how Abraham understood that religion worked. The gods demanded that which was most valuable to you. If you didn't give it, you'd pay the price. That's what the world was like at that time.

So Abraham sets out, and, *"he reaches the place on the third day."*

He and his son travel for three days. It is three days in which his son is as good as dead. When they get to the mountain, what does Abraham say to the servants? He says to them, *"Stay here with the donkey while the boy and I go over there. We will worship and then we will come back to you."*

What? Abraham is going to offer his son, right? That's what the story is about, correct? God tells Abraham to offer his son, and he does so—or at least proves that he would do so—that's the point, isn't it?

But what Abraham says to the servants is that he's going to go offer his son, and then come back with his son. Clearly there is something else going on in this story, just below the surface. The story is subverting itself, begging you to see something far more significant going on.

As they walk up the mountain, Isaac asks Abraham where the sacrifice will come from. In the standard reading of the story, he's going to his death *because his dad loves God so much.* But we've already seen Abraham tip his hand that something else is up. So we're not buying that angle.

What is Abraham's answer? *God himself will provide.*

How clever! It's a non-answer answer. Abraham is in on the joke, or whatever it is that you'd call it.

Then Abraham gets ready to offer his son, but he doesn't because God stops him and then he offers a ram instead. End of story.

Except that it isn't the end.

An angel shows up and says that Abraham is going to be blessed and, *"through your offspring all nations on earth will be blessed. . . ."*

So, back to our original question: What kind of God would ask a man to sacrifice his son?

Now, an answer: Not this one.

The other gods may demand your firstborn, but not this God.

So if God doesn't want Abraham to offer his son, why the charade?

Several responses:

First, the drama is the point. Abraham knows what to do when he's told to offer his son because this is always where religion heads toward. So at first, this God appears to be like all the other gods. The story, at first, seems to be like the other stories about gods who are never satisfied. The first audience for this story would have heard this before, and it would have been familiar. But then it's not. The story takes a shocking turn which comes out of nowhere. This God disrupts the familiarity of the story by interrupting the sacrifice. Picture an early audience gasping. What? This God *stopped* the sacrifice? Huh? The gods don't do that!

Second, the God in this story *provides*. Worship and sacrifice was about *you* giving to the *gods*. Yet *this* story is about *this* God giving to *Abraham*. A God who gives? Who provides?

Third, this isn't a story about what Abraham does for God, it's a story about what God does for Abraham. Mind blowing. New. Ground breaking. A story about a God who doesn't demand anything, but gives and blesses.

Fourth, Abraham is told that God is just getting started, and that this God is going to bless Abraham with such love and favor that through Abraham everyone on earth is going to also be blessed. This God isn't angry or demanding or unleashing wrath. This God has intentions to bless everyone. Abraham is invited to trust, have faith, believe, and to live in these promises.

Can you see how many game changing ideas are in this one story? Can you see why people told this story? Can you see why it endured? Can you think of any other stories about a son who was as good as dead for three days, but then lived in such a way that the story about him confronted the conventional wisdom of the day, and the gods are angry and demanding with the insistence that God blesses and gives and provides?

All that's left for us to do is to know and trust in our God who is really like that . . . and so much more.

11

Prayer for the Beginning of Lent

Pope John XXIII

O Lord Jesus, you who at the beginning of your public life withdrew into the desert, we beg you to teach all men that recollection of mind which is the beginning of conversion and salvation.

Leaving your home at Nazareth and your sweet Mother, you wished to experience solitude, weariness, and hunger. To the tempter who proposed to you the trial of miracles, you replied with the strength of eternal wisdom, in itself a miracle of heavenly grace.

It is Lent.

O Lord, do not let us turn to "broken cisterns," which can hold no water (Jeremiah 2:13), nor imitate the unfaithful servant or the foolish virgins; do not let us be so blinded by the enjoyment of the good things of earth that our hearts become insensible to the cry of the poor, of the sick, of orphan children, and of those innumerable brothers of ours who still lack the necessary minimum to eat, to clothe their nakedness, and to gather their family together under one roof.

You also, O Jesus, were immersed in the river of Jordan, under the eyes of the crowd, although very few then were able to recognize you; and this mystery of tardy faith, or of indifference, prolonged through the centuries, is a source of grief for those who love you and have received the mission of making you known in the world.

O grant to the successors of your apostles and disciples and to all who call themselves after your Name and your Cross, to press on with the work of spreading the Gospel and bear witness to it in prayer, suffering, and loving obedience to your will!

And since you, an innocent lamb, came before John in the attitude of a sinner, so draw us also to the waters of the Jordan. To the Jordan will we go to confess our sins and cleanse our souls. And as the skies opened to announce the voice of your Father, expressing his pleasure in you, so, having successfully overcome our trial and lived austerely through the forty days of our Lent, may we, O Jesus, when the day of your Resurrection dawns, hear once more in our innermost hearts the same heavenly Father's voice, recognizing us as his children.

O holy Lent of this mystic year of the Ecumenical Council! May this prayer rise, on this evening of serene religious recollection, from every house where people work, love, and suffer. May the angels of heaven gather the prayers of all the souls of little children, of generous-hearted young men and women, of hard-working and self-sacrificing parents, and of all who suffer in body and mind, and present their prayers to God. From him will flow down in abundance the gifts of his heavenly joys, of which our Apostolic Benediction is a pledge and a reflection.

12

Catch Me in My Scurrying

Ted Loder

Catch me in my mindless scurrying, Lord,
and hold me in this Lenten season:
hold my spirit to the beacon of your grace
and grant me light enough to walk boldly,
to feel passionately,
to love aggressively;
grant me peace enough to want more,
to work for more
and to submit to nothing less,
and to fear only you . . .
only you!
Bequeath me not becalmed seas,
slack sails and premature benedictions,
but breathe into me a torment,

ALL SHALL BE WELL

storm enough to make within myself
and from myself,
something . . .
something new,
something saving,
something true,
a gladness of heart,
a pitch for a song in the storm,
a word of praise lived,
a gratitude shared,
a cross dared,
a joy received. . . .

13

ﶩ

Not Servants, but Friends

Mother Mary Joseph Rogers, MM

For forty days, we follow Christ to His cross. Are we going to follow as onlookers, or are we going to be real companions to Christ? This is the question we should all ask ourselves. Jesus has called us friends and says: *"You are not servants, but friends."* Now, a friend is a person to whom we can look under all circumstances for understanding, consolation, sympathy, and help. The reproaches that are heaped on our friend fall also on us, and we hear Jesus, in the words of the Psalmist, saying: *"I have expected reproach and misery, and I looked for one that would grieve together with Me, but there was none; and for one that would comfort Me, and I found none"* (Psalm 68, vv. 21–22). Now let this not be true of us. We, by our very presence here, have even said to the world that we are the friends of Christ. Let us, therefore, be Jesus' real companions . . . particularly with him during these days of sorrow.

That is the time we need friends, and that is the time when we, ourselves, if we have friends, yearn to give to them. . . . Now in order to help us to be close to Christ during Lent, let us each pick out some phase of the Passion that makes a particular appeal to us. Let us use that very religiously as the subject of our meditations. Let it become the pivotal thought of our actions. Then, let us take secondly, some fault that we wish to overcome, or a virtue that we wish to acquire or which we wish to strengthen, and examine each in the light of this phase of the Passion we have chosen, and let us go through Lent, trying to eradicate our fault by what we learn during our meditation on the Passion. . . . And so, Sisters, I wish you a very holy and a very happy Lent, because we are happy in proportion as we sacrifice ourselves.

February 27, 1938

~

14

The Temptations in the Wilderness

(LUKE 4:1–13)

Ernesto Cardenal

We read how Jesus was taken to the wilderness by the Holy Spirit and there spent forty days fasting, and I said that this simply meant that Jesus probably had a period of retreat in one of those Essene communities, reflecting about his mission through prayer and fasting.

> *And afterward he felt hunger. Then the devil said to him: "If you really are the Son of God, command this stone to turn into bread." Jesus answered him: "The Scripture says, 'Man does not live by bread alone, but also by every word that God speaks.'"*

FRANCISCO: "The devil wanted him to perform a senseless, useless miracle that wouldn't do anybody any good."

OLIVIA: "Or that would do good only for Jesus himself. Later he would perform the miracle of giving bread to a whole crowd, but that was different. Here we were dealing with a selfish miracle."

GUSTAVO: "And I see that more than anything else the temptation consisted in reducing his messianism to a purely material level—a developmentalist messianism. Of course, bread is important, but we can't stop there. Revolution doesn't mean just giving food and clothing and comforts to people. It goes beyond that. And this was a temptation that Jesus had as the Messiah, and he rejected it."

TOMAS: "Bread is food. Animals live only on food. People live on another food too: the bread of love, or the words of these meetings that we're having here, I mean the Eucharist."

MANUEL: "Christ says that food isn't enough for human life. Just like animals can't live without food, people can't be truly human without the word of God. Without it a person isn't human like other people. He's an animal, a wolf. . . ."

ELVIS: "To teach us that, that we need the word of

God for life, he had gone into the wilderness to fast."

MARCELINO: "The word of God gives us bread too. Because in a community some might have bread and others might not. And if there's love we share it and we all eat. If there isn't any love, even though there's a lot of food people will be hungry because a few people will hoard the food."

OSCAR: "The word that God speaks is love, because that's the message God has given us and Christ brought to earth."

We went on to the second temptation. The devil takes Jesus to a very high mountain and shows him all the kingdoms of the earth. This is something that he must have seen in his imagination, I said.

And the devil said to him: "I will give you all this power and the greatness of these kingdoms. For I have received all this and I give it to anybody I choose. If you will kneel down and worship me, it will all be yours."

LAUREANO: "He's like a politician, that devil. Because that's what political campaigns are like. A man comes into a town and makes all kinds of promises so people will vote for him. And people do vote for him and afterwards he doesn't give them shit."

Another says: "The devil wanted Jesus to adore him so he could be God."

And another: "He was offering him an imperialist messianism."

"Then imperialism would be all right if it was the imperialism of Jesus?" asked JULIO.

FELIPE: "No, because if Jesus had fallen into temptation his imperialism would have been just like the others."

TOMAS: "Just like theirs, because they're under the power of the devil."

TOÑO: "There's one thing here: The devil is making him a false proposal. He tells Jesus that he's going to give him all the power and the riches of the world, and Jesus, by refusing, is stating that the true master is himself, that is, all of humanity. And he doesn't have to adore the devil to get him to give Jesus what is rightly his. And that's our situation, too."

I said: "Why do you suppose the devil says that he has received all this?"

WILLIAM: "He grabbed it all. It's a dictatorship. He has the power, but a power that's not legitimate. It's stolen. Imperialism and capitalism and all oppression belong to him. It's up to us to take from the devil what he has grabbed for himself—the riches of the earth. This temptation of Jesus is also a picture of what's happening now: Those in power offer things to the people so that they'll serve them. . . ."

FRANCISCO: "And from what we see in this passage, all governments are of the devil. Christ couldn't set up a government like that. He came to make a Revolution against all these powers. And there will have to come a day when there isn't any government. Then the Revolution will be a complete success."

And FELIPE said: "The devil declares that he is the owner of the kingdoms of the earth. This must be because when he was condemned the devil fell into the depths of the earth, into the abyss. And so he believes he's the owner of the earth. It's not true, but he thinks he owns it. And he wants it all for himself, like a dictator, like an exploiter. And everybody who wants to take over the earth is like the devil. But they don't own the earth, because the only way to own the earth, it seems to me, is in little lots—and little lots all equal."

ALEJANDRO: "When the devil showed Christ in the spirit all the countries he must have been showing him the cities and the governments. Not the lakes, the mountains, the volcanoes, because they aren't evil, they don't belong to the devil."

MARCELINO: "Power. All power is evil and it comes from the devil."

TOMAS: "The devil offers him all this so that he'll adore him, I mean so that he'll become haughty and selfish, so that he'll go over to his side."

I said: "It's true, the devil is the master of pride, of haughtiness, of the power of people over people. This is his nature, and this is what he gives to his people. That's what he offers to Jesus and Jesus rejects it."

Someone else comments: "Riches don't belong to the devil. It's the selfishness of the rich—that belongs to him."

Afterwards the devil took him to the city of Jerusalem and he took him up to the highest point of the temple and he said to him: "If you are truly the Son of God, cast yourself down from here; because in the Scripture it says: 'God will order his angels to take care of you . . .'"

TOMAS: "The devil told him to fly off the roof of the temple because he didn't have faith that he was the Son of God. He wanted to know if he was or wasn't. That's why he said that to him."

OSCAR MAIRENA: "The fact is that the devil was testing him out: If you really are, throw yourself down."

Another said: "He's suspicious."

And another: "He's confident. What's happening is that he wants to control the Son of God, to have more power than him, and so he gives him orders to see if he obeys. And so we see the great power that he has in the world . . ."

And the journalist PEDRO RAFAEL GUTIERREZ, who once had a top position on a government newspaper and who now lives with us: "I see a picture here too: The devil took Jesus up, just as he seizes many of us and lifts us into certain positions. It says: 'He seized him and he took him up.' So to some he gives riches, he gives power, he gives greatness. And once these people are powerful then comes the temptation to screw the weak, to oppress them. And he said: 'No, don't tempt me!' As I see it, there is a temptation of the devil, which is to raise people up, to lift us to the heights and then let us fall."

JULIO MAIRENA: "And it's a useless miracle that the devil proposes: to throw himself down and have angels save him. What for? That wouldn't do anyone any good. That was a show-off temptation."

WILLIAM: "As I see it, this is a messianic temptation too. Throwing himself down from the temple without anything happening to him would be spectacular. Imagine if it was on a feast day and all the people were gathered there. And he presented himself as the Messiah dazzling the masses with his miracle. And Jesus refused to be this kind of a Messiah. Later he would go to Jerusalem during the feast, but in a different way. He rejected the temptation: He told the devil to go to hell. But the Gospel says the devil 'went away for sometime. . . .' Afterwards the bastard came back."

"Yes," I said, "in fact these three temptations are a single temptation: that Jesus present himself as the commanding and triumphant Messiah that the Jews were waiting for. And this would be a real temptation for him. And he rejected it, knowing that liberation for him had to come through suffering and death. When the Jews asked him for a great spectacular sign, he told them that the only sign he would give them was that of Jonah (his death and resurrection). And this temptation not to accept his passion and death, to be another kind of Messiah, he would have it again in Gethsemane."

FELIPE PEÑA: "I see that the devil tempts him by saying 'because the Scriptures say.' It's just like a lot of Catholics and Protestants use the Bible to defend their interests. They say: 'The Scriptures say such and such a thing. . . .' And it's all to exploit us."

And another: "It's like when they say to the poor: 'You've got to respect the property of the rich because it comes to them from God.'"

And still another: "And there's another temptation too: not doing anything, thinking all you have to do is pray, like a lot of Catholics believe; or read the Bible and be very religious, like a lot of Protestants believe."

Jesus returned to Galilee filled with the Holy Spirit, and there was talk about him in all the region around.

ALEJANDRO: "He went to the wilderness guided by the Holy Spirit, and there he was filled more with the Holy Spirit—with this retreat that he had with God, and with the temptations that he overcame. He came back with more love, that's what 'filled with the Holy Spirit' means. He was convinced that he had to be humble and poor to be the liberator of the poor. The devil had tried to make him dizzy with greatness. . . ."

TOMAS: "He received more of the Holy Spirit so that he could suffer and bear it, I mean because of what he was going to suffer at the time of his death."

And I said it was interesting to see that when he was filled with the Holy Spirit, he set out on no other journey, began no other project. Instead he returned to his home, to the humble people where he had been brought up.

ᵏᵉ

Final Sanity

Phyllis Tickle

The forty penitential weekdays and six Sundays that follow Mardi Gras and precede Easter are the days of greatest calm in the church's year. Since by long centuries of custom the date of Easter is annually determined from the first Sunday after the full moon on or after March 21, the intertwining of physical and spiritual seasons is virtually inevitable. The resulting union of deep winter and holy preparation makes reflection, even penitence, a natural activity.

One night years ago, toward the end of winter, there was a storm, a cold front shifting suddenly and dropping onto us with ferocity and winds that bent down the pine trees along the fence line. Sometime after I went to bed, it tore open the pasture gate. We awoke the next morning to bitter cold and a scattered herd: two pregnant heifers in the front yard, six more in the garden eating up what was left of the turnip greens, and seven others, mostly yearlings, playing at some kind of heifer tag in the windy orchard.

The mud from the previous month's snow was three inches thick. Even frozen, it came laughing up to suck off our boots. We slipped and fell and prodded swollen bellies until, ourselves covered with ooze, we fell onto the broken gate and laughed out loud to the gray dawn skies and the startled blackbirds. We drove the last cows through finally, my son John and I, and repaired the gate right enough, coming in out of the cold with feet so wet and frozen that we couldn't feel them, our nightclothes covered in the half-thawed manure. We stank up the kitchen with the good stench of late winter and of the earth when it is resisting one last cold front with the heat of coming fertility.

Later I stood at the spigot and washed the mud from our boots and felt again, as I do every year at this season, a grief for the passing cold. Looking across the pastures to the pond below, I knew it had indeed been the last storm before the spring, and I wanted to run backward toward the early morning, toward the winds and breaking limbs of the previous night.

"*Lenzin*," our German ancestors used to call this season, and since then we have called it "Lent." It is a time when Christians decorate stone churches with the sea's color and wrap their priests in the mollusk's purple. It was once a time when all things passed through the natural depression of seclusion, short food supplies, and inactivity, a time when body and land both rested. It is still, in the country, a final sanity before the absurd wastefulness of spring.

Each year at this time it is harder for me to desire butterflies and lilies, even to wish for resurrection. Each year I come a little closer to needing the dullness of the sky and the rarity of a single redheaded woodpecker knocking for grubs in the pine bark. Each year also I come a little closer to the single-mindedness of the drake who, muddy underside showing, waddles now across the ice to the cold center water to wash himself for his mate, all in the hope of ducklings later on.

That year, through the thin, sharp air I could hear the younger children in the barn. They were building tunnels again, making forts from the dried bales of hay. From the yapping I knew that even the dogs had joined in the intricacies that the children's imaginations had contrived. Five-year-old Rebecca chased field mice as her brothers built forts. She would catch another soon and drown it in the water trough with unsullied sadism, feeling only the accomplishment that came from having helped to keep her part of the world in balance.

In the summer, the mice would leave, going back to the fields again, and she would take to pulling everything that bloomed instead, bringing them all in to me indiscriminately. The tin-roofed barn would be stifling, and the hay forts would have all been eaten. The boys would be picking beans and complaining of the itch from the okra leaves, being themselves too hot and tired to desire anything except nightfall and bed. The drake would have a family, which he would abandon to the mate he had so much desired, and the woodpecker's carmine head would burn out to tired tan.

The farm in the summer becomes like the city is all year: too much color, too much noise, too much growing, too much hurry to stave off loss and destruction, too little natural death and gentle ending, too little time for play, too little pointless imagination.

I can remember many summers now; it is the singular advantage of years that one can do so. And I remember that once summer comes, I spend it wallowing in the easiness of it—the excess of its fruits and vegetables, the companionship of summer's constant sounds as the hum of the insects and of the rototillers give way in the evening to the croaking of the frogs and the raucousness of the katydids. I remember also how I would begin early, in that green time of Ordinary Time, to dread the stillness of the coming cold, to fear the weariness of winter menus, the bitterness of breaking open pond water for thirsty cattle, and the packing of lunches—interminable lunches—for reluctant children on their way to school.

But now, years later, it is Lent once again, and for one more snow I can luxuriate in the isolation of the cold, attend laconically to who I am, what I value, and why I'm here. Religion has always kept earth time. Liturgy only gives sanction to what the heart already knows.

16

A Complicated Grief

Kerry Weber

When my cell phone rings early one sunny fall morning, I reach for it groggily, see that the call is from my mother, and know that whatever she is about to say will be heartbreaking. I am still in bed in my pajamas, and my mom tells me that Marian Elizabeth has been born. Everything else my mother says is drowned out by the roar in my brain that tells me that I must see my new niece. "Call me back on FaceTime," I say interrupting her. A moment later, the video call comes through.

Marian Elizabeth, named for two women with difficult and miraculous pregnancies, is wearing a hat that is way too big for her tiny body, two months premature. My sister, Elizabeth, is holding her daughter both gingerly and with such strong love. And I just keep saying over and over again, "She's so beautiful, I love you both so much. You are both so beautiful. I love you. I love you. She is beautiful," even though I know my niece can't fully comprehend it, while at the same time trying to understand it all myself. And then a few minutes later, somehow, I tear myself away from the phone, and I head off to work, and I wait.

I am waiting for the next, inevitable call. The joy of seeing my niece alive is accompanied by the heaviness of knowing that what we had expected had, in fact, come to pass. Marian, facing a host of health problems, will only live for a few hours. This first time seeing my niece will also be my last. During those hours of her life, Marian is baptized in a tiny white garment that swims around her, while I pore over manuscripts at my desk until I get a message telling me that my niece has died.

We first learn about the complications with my sister's pregnancy on Mother's Day weekend. My sister is rushed to the doctor, and the doctors think she may be having a miscarriage. She is put on bed rest until she can go back to the doctor on Monday to find out if the baby still has a heartbeat. "All we can do is pray," my family keeps saying, though I am not always sure if saying such things means that we're resigned to our seeming helplessness or attempting one last-ditch effort for control. I know that prayer can change the way we look at a situation, but I don't care about that at the moment; I just want my prayer to change the outcome.

I pray that her suffering, her child's suffering, be transferred, in some material way, to me. I want this all to work like it does when I go hiking and my boyfriend offers to carry more of our supplies because then we can walk farther together.

Monday morning comes, and we learn that the baby's heartbeat has been found. And then we learn the rest. We learn, gradually, of the numerous, potentially lethal developmental and health problems that the baby faces or will face if she makes it into this world. The doctors still are not even sure the baby will reach full term. And if she does, the doctors are increasingly certain she will not live beyond a few hours. The situation seems like a cruel response to my prayer, a kind of bait and switch. My sister and her husband decide that they will love this kid for whatever time they've got. And again, we wait.

In early September, my sister is hugely pregnant, due to complications, even though the baby is still so small. Every time I look at her, I am reminded anew of what is and what likely will be soon. And life and death seem so close, and her whole house seems pregnant with both terrifying ambiguity and unlikely hope.

In the Letter of James we read (1:2):

> Consider it all joy, my brothers, when you encounter various trials, for you know that the testing of your faith produces perseverance. And let perseverance be perfect, so that you may be perfect and complete, lacking in nothing.

This phrase—the testing of your faith—can be an odd one to parse, implying, it seems, that God sits on some gilded throne in a heavenly science lab taking notes on how we react to certain stimuli. I can't believe that. Yet there is no doubt that suffering does test us. It forces us to figure out why we keep going, what we should rely on. And I have to believe that while God is not making clinical notes, God is taking note. Even when it feels as though we are alone, God sees us being changed by suffering. And even more than that, God accompanies us. God accompanies us through that pain, through the numbness, through the disbelief and the unbelief.

The natural question when we encounter suffering is: Why? But sometimes the more helpful one is: Where? Where am I being called by this suffering? Where can I find a supportive community? Where is God in all of this? Because, as James suggests, we have to persevere.

So often we tell ourselves that we should not complain about the minor inconveniences or even significant trials in our own lives when so much "real" suffering is going on in the world. It only seems right to persevere in our lives grateful for what we have, even if that means being grateful for calm and beautiful deaths. As a wise priest once said to me: "All suffering is real." Every life is precious. The grief caused by the death of one child is not immediately alleviated because we know that elsewhere, in places of war or poverty, thousands of others have also died. And the suffering of those children has weight far beyond its use in putting our own seemingly more fortunate lives in perspective.

Yet when we hear or tell of others' suffering we experience a little bit of it. We suffer with, as Christ did for us, entering into our imperfect world. St. Ignatius calls us, in the third week of the Spiritual Exercises, to consider Christ's suffering from the Last Supper through the Garden of Gethsemane. And in doing so, he says that we should want, even ask "for grief with Christ in grief, anguish with Christ in anguish, tears and interior pain at such great pain which Christ suffered for me." This isn't easy.

Marian's funeral is one of the most horrible and beautiful experiences of my life, at once tragic and grace-filled. I arrive at the small, familiar chapel with my parents, and Elizabeth and her husband arrive separately, a reminder that as much as my parents and siblings and I are still family, my sister now is a part of her own little family. She looks so somber and so strong and still young but wears a more weathered expression, like someone who has been at sea for a long time and is still getting used to land again. The casket is tiny, maybe two feet long, and white, and it has a heart embossed in the top, and it sits in the front of the chapel covered by the tiny baptismal garment that once enveloped Marian's body. And as heartbreaking as it is to see the casket carried in by the man from the funeral parlor, it is more heartbreaking to see it as my sister and her husband carry it out together after the liturgy, walking while swaying with grief, and singing and crying. The casket looks so light, not like the heaviness we expect on that final journey out. But by far the most heartbreaking moment comes early in the Mass, as I watch my mother looking at my sister looking at that casket, both faces stricken with grief on behalf of their daughters.

Perhaps God does not bargain with our lives the way I had tried to. Perhaps my prayer should not have been to suffer instead of my sister but to suffer with, to truly exist compassionately, to have asked for "grief with her grief and anguish with her anguish." We cannot always take away someone's suffering, but we can walk beside them, help them carry their burdens and in that way be able to walk farther together.

And, if I cannot always, as James asks, see all of it as joy, perhaps I can at least find a way to see the moments of joy in the pain, the grace and kindness of the doctors who treated my sister, the priest who slept in the hospital waiting room in order to baptize the baby at a moment's notice.

Painful suffering, monumental moments, can divide life into a before and an after. Yet we must persevere; we continue on, if differently. It takes time to process suffering. Hope and joy look different. In Paul's Second Letter to the Corinthians we read:

> We are afflicted in every way, but not con-
> strained; perplexed, but not driven to despair
> . . . always carrying about in the body the dy-
> ing of Jesus, so that the life of Jesus may also
> be manifested in our body.

How miraculous, how perfect, that in each of us we harbor both the living and dying Christ. In each of us, at all times, a million Good Fridays and Resurrections. And maybe those days in between, as well. We forget about those days sometimes, days during which the apostles must have been afraid and alone and the world seemed dark and no one knew what would happen next.

During times of suffering, no matter how many times we are told that a resurrection is coming, it is tough to believe that we will emerge from the darkness, that we will eventually find that tomb empty and hear our equivalent of "He is no longer here!" How hard it can be to believe that eventually we will find a new moment when hope and joy look different, yet again.

And so, instead of wondering why, we simply persevere, we try to find that joy, to let it transform us and to simply love our way through it all. Because even in our worst moments, this is what God does for us. God loves us back from the edge. God looks at us and says, "You are so beautiful, I love you so much. You are so beautiful. I love you. I love you. You are beautiful." Even though God knows we cannot fully comprehend.

17

A Lifetime Job

Dorothy Day

"Hell is not to love anymore," writes George Bernanos in *The Diary of a Country Priest*. I felt when I read this that the blackness of hell must indeed have descended on Our Lord in His agony.

The one thing that makes our work easier most certainly is the love we bear for each other and for the people for whom we work. The work becomes difficult only when there is quarreling and dissension and when one's own heart is filled with a spirit of criticism.

In the past, when I have spoken on the necessity of mutual charity, of self-criticism rather than criticism of others, the accusation has been made that I talk to the men as though they were angels, that I do not see their faults. Which is certainly not true.

The difficulty for me is not in *not* seeing the other person's faults, but in seeing and developing his virtues. A community of lay people is entirely different from a religious community like the Benedictines. We must imitate them by thinking in terms of work and prayer. But we must always remember that those who come to us are not here voluntarily, many of them, but because of economic circumstances. They have taken refuge with us. There is the choice of being on the streets, taking city care such as it is, or staying with us. Even many of the young "leaders" who give up home and position to come to help in the work are the rebel type and often undisciplined. Their great virtues often mean correspondingly great faults.

Yet those who are interested in the movement fail to see why it does not run as smoothly as a religious movement. They expect our houses and farms to be governed as a religious community is ruled, and in general they take the attitude that I am the one in authority who should rule with an iron hand, the others accepting this willingly. Truly the position of authority is the difficult one.

One of the difficulties of the work is to find those who are willing to assume authority. Leaders are hard to find. The very best in our groups, members of unions for instance, are steadfast, humble, filled with the love of God and their fellows, and their very virtues make it hard for them to assume leadership. Often, then, they leave it to the articulate ones who are often most articulate about the wrongdoings of others. They leave the foremost positions to those who like to talk rather than to do, to those who are aggressive and pugnacious and who do the movement harm rather than good. If they are not saying the wrong thing, enunciating the wrong ideas—being politicians, in other words—then they are saying but not doing, and even doing contrary to what they are saying.

It is human to dislike being found fault with. If you point out faults, rather than point out the better way of doing things, then the sting is there, and resentments and inactivity are the results. "What's the use of anything, it's all wrong." Such childishness! But human beings are like that, and we must recognize their faults and try in every possible way to bring out their virtues.

On a visit to a group, there are always a half-dozen who are filled with complaints. If you try to turn their criticisms so as to change their attitude of mind, you are "refusing to listen" to them. You don't give them a chance to show you how wrong everything is. You don't know what is going on. It is in vain that you assure them you do know what is going on, just how faulty different ones have been. No, that is not enough, if you treat all with equal patience. Then you are not paying any attention to the complaints. Positive work to overcome obstacles such as people's temperaments is not enough for the fault-finders. They want recriminations and reprimands. "You are going to let him get away with that?" is the cry, when you try with courtesy and sympathy and respect to draw people together and induce cooperation.

It is very trying to receive so many complaints and not to be able to do anything about them. Those who do not complain and who try to work along the positive method are accused of being yes-men, and those who tell on each other and who always have some tale of woe are informers. So in either case there is trouble.

Oh yes, my dear comrades, and fellow workers, I see only too clearly how bad things are with us all, how bad you all are, and how bad a leader I am. I see it only too often and only too clearly. It is because I see it so clearly that I must lift up my head and keep in sight the aims we must always hold before us. I must see the large and generous picture of the new social order wherein justice dwelleth. I must hold always in mind the new earth where God's Will will be done as it is in heaven. I must hold it in mind for my own courage and for yours.

The new social order as it could be and would be if all men loved God and loved their brothers because they are all sons of God! A land of peace and tranquility and joy in work and activity. It is heaven indeed that we are contemplating. Do you expect that we are going to be able to accomplish it here? We can accomplish much, of that I am certain. We can do much to change the face of the earth, in that I have hope and faith. But these pains and sufferings are the price we have to pay. Can we change men in a night or a day? Can we give them as much as three months or even a year? A child is forming in the mother's womb for nine long months, and it seems so long. But to make a man in the time of our present disorder with all the world convulsed with hatred and strife and selfishness, that is a lifetime's work and then too often it is not accomplished.

Even the best of human love is filled with self-seeking. To work to increase our love for God and for our fellow man (and the two must go hand in hand), this is a lifetime job. We are never going to be finished.

Love and ever more love is the only solution to every problem that comes up. If we love each other enough, we will bear with each other's faults and burdens. If we love enough, we are going to light that fire in the hearts of others. And it is love that will burn out the sins and hatreds that sadden us. It is love that will make us want to do great things for each other. No sacrifice and no suffering will then seem too much.

Yes, I see only too clearly how bad people are. I wish I did not see it so. It is my own sins that give me such clarity. If I did not bear the scars of so many sins to dim my sight and dull my capacity for love and joy, then I would see Christ more clearly in you all.

I cannot worry much about your sins and miseries when I have so many of my own. I can only love you all, poor fellow travelers, fellow sufferers. I do not want to add one least straw to the burden you already carry. My prayer from day to day is that God will so enlarge my heart that I will see you all, and live with you all, in His love.

18

Flaw

Joe Hoover

If you have ever thrown an elbow or slid cleats high.

If you have ever snapped back or punched first.

If you have ever quietly stolen inconsequential things, small pieces of candy from a store, a magazine from a waiting room.

If you have wiped your mouth on a dishtowel and hung it back up.

If you have argued from authority.

If you don't wash your hands, not much.

If you decided somewhere along the way—without even realizing it—that you would not have a relationship with the plaintive, pith-helmeted mail carrier. Instead you two would walk by each other day after day like creatures from a sad divorce eons ago who had forgotten they ever knew each other.

If you fail to give waitstaff irresistible small talk like you used to when you were twenty-three and your charm was the only saleable thing on your resume.

If you walk by figures sleeping on the concrete under rough gray blankets and quietly wonder where they screwed up to get themselves there; and then feel incredibly judgmental for thinking such things. And then wondering again: really, what did they do?

If vertical lines have formed between your eyebrows from a lifetime of looking at people with suspicion.

If you lack enthusiasm for the talents of others but instead let their despicable gifts swarm over you like man-eating knifefish.

If some reasonable cleric ever told you that in Greek the word "sin" means "missing the mark," and you turned that into a kind of a general pass for yourself. As if somehow all the inane, corrupt, or just mildly sad things you do could be melted down and written off into a darts allegory.

If you have ever felt that you were kind of too good for this, and this could be anything.

If you are a resolute pacifist in regard to wars you aren't even invited to, but undertake silent acts of violence against any number of people who flash into your mind all day long.

If you do not think you are allowed three consecutive moments of honest anger.

If you meet every slight, each missed appointment, every unreturned phone call, with it's alright, or you were probably busy, or a quick look away and no worries; and so melt away bit by bit into people's dim consciousness of you as one whose time or expectations are not really to be taken seriously.

If you let slip into conversations with friends that you haven't visited a doctor in seven years. And you say this while hoping someone will scold you and order you to make an appointment and offer to drive you herself. And when they never do, converting this into state's evidence number 76 why the powers of the world have in quiet indifference arrayed themselves against you.

If you still long to tell people your ACT score.

Or if you humbly refuse to tell them your ACT score when they ask, saying only, I don't want to boast, you guys, don't want to boast.

If there is a hint of irony or sarcasm in everything you do and thus no one feels like they know you. And not in the way that we are all ultimately unknowable, as God is unknowable, and all sentient beings blessed into the dirt of conventional reality are unknowable. But unknowable as in, just, we wish we knew you a little.

If you seem not to have become the man you wanted to be because . . . because . . . you're lazy. And it is not your dad's fault or the world's fault or low blood sugar or a failure to ingrain into the depths of your soul like some Kendrick Lamar hook the fact that God loves you—but because you are thirty-two and very talented and very smart and you play a stupendous amount of video games.

If you are a heroic and beloved ghetto nurse or teacher or poet revolutionary, and don't understand why the people who actually live with you can barely put up with you. And assume it is because, sadly enough, they are probably jealous.

If someone ever told you—dogmatically or not—that the thin silver computer you carry in your messenger bag uses up more energy, from conception to natural death, than a car; or that recycling aluminum cans inflicts as much misery unto the earth as the equivalent misery they would imbue in a landfill, and you just wanted right there on the spot to give up the whole blessed enterprise.

If you are really, honestly, just not very nice. Not to anybody.

If you meet with lawyers and sign papers and pack boxes and are still unable to admit that you and your wife are getting a divorce.

If you have had little injections of disease into those lines between your eyebrows, and your clever religious daughter told you that just as Christ became sin in order to redeem mankind, you have become botulinum toxin in order to redeem your face.

If your rent payments are late because you don't believe in rent, but you still have an apartment that has rent payments.

If you don't think much of yourself. If you believe, frankly, that you are pretty much a dirtbag. And just saying that actually gives you a sense of relief. But then that relief does not melt away the fact that you still think you are a dirtbag.

If you pay occasional witness from a newspaper to distant wars, to their IED's and casualty lists, their market squares and holy festivals blown to pieces, to the small photos of stony-faced dead kids from Oklahoma, and wonder why the whole thing doesn't seem to worm its way one inch into your heart.

If every time you start talking about other people you begin by pointing out that you don't usually talk about other people.

If your quest for moral perfection is slowly killing you.

If you do any of this, or any of it is done to you—the flaws, the sins, the marks missed; an unhinged world pressed on your soul, or your unhinged sins visited on the world; if this is the case, then this church season of Lent has been for you. This season, and this week, and its charred days; days with prefixes, Spy, Holy, Good, Holy. These days are for you not even because you are necessarily Catholic, or Christian, or believe in God or saints or crucifixes as scaffolding constructed for the dismantling of all wrongs. But because other people do.

And those other people take time to name these wrongs. They name them and so, like Adam and his beasts, have some dominion over them. Through incense and kneelers and soft lulling chants they are grounding down, getting into the deep sadness of themselves. Putting their conscience through its paces. And something about Jesus, and something about redemption. Something about laying all on the king.

But first taking firm hold of the flaws, no matter how small, and gazing in confusion and sorrow and wonder.

ᴥ

A Sign of Life

Donald McQuade, MM

It has been said that the blood of martyrs is the seed of the Church. In other words persecution and martyrdom in the Church paradoxically bring her new and deeper life in Christ, for through her suffering the Church is intimately joined to the passion and death of Jesus—and therefore to his resurrection.

Throughout this century there have been countless Christian men and women martyred for their faith—in concentration camps, in prisons, in their homes and even, as with Bishop Oscar Romero in El Salvador—the altar while he was saying Mass. Here in the Philippines how many unknown catechists and lay workers, besides priests, have been "salvaged" (killed) or have just disappeared?

We live in an age of persecution and martyrdom in

the Church and there is some feeling that it will increase in coming years. This modern attempt to silence and kill the Church, as with the earlier Roman persecution, is actually a sign of her life for, like Jesus himself, the Church today is undergoing the paschal mystery of suffering and dying before coming to new life.

Jesus tells us that:

> If the world hates you, remember that it hated me before you. If you belonged to the world, the world would love you as its own; but because you do not belong to the world, because my choice withdrew you from the world, therefore the world hates you. Remember the words I say to you: a servant is not greater than his master. If they persecuted me, they will persecute you too; if they kept my word, they will keep yours as well.
>
> —John 15:18-20

Paradoxically, these seemingly foreboding words are in reality a sign that the Church is living the gospel well enough in our times to warrant persecution—and thus even more life. Living in an age of martyrs, we live in an age of life.

🖎

20

Bald Places

Hob Osterlund

Rooms 652 and 653 couldn't be more different, except they're both bald.

Room 652 is a woman with a glioblastoma. It's the kind of brain tumor that often kills fast, usually within six months of diagnosis. She's fifty-seven. Her name is Teea. *The doctor says I'm history*, says Teea softly, without apparent fear. Her humor is deceptive. I bet she'd bribe, threaten, or supplicate all creatures, medical or otherwise, two-legged or four, who promised they could buy her even one extra week. She wants to live so bad she could scream it to the heavenly rafters, but she doesn't, at least not in the hospital. She behaves calmly here.

Each of her three daughters is as beautiful as their mama, even though radiation therapy fried the hair right off their mama's head. She only has curly clumps above her ears now, like a clown. *I'm thinking of having them bronzed*, she says, so she can put the last follicular evidence from the upper end of her body on her mantle above the fireplace, next to her baby boots. Nobody remarks that the boots are from the beginning of her life and the hair is likely to be from the end of it.

The oldest daughter is studying primates somewhere in Africa and came home two days after her grandmother telephoned. The middle daughter's in the air force, training to be a pilot. The youngest lives nearby, her dancer's body temporarily compromised by an unexpected pregnancy offered as a goodbye gift from a yoga instructor. All are with their mother in the hospital as regular as rain.

Teea figures the lion's share of her own parenting duties are behind her, and she wants to sit back on some padded chaise lounge, drink a nice Australian wine, and watch her daughters do what they do best. She wants to be the audience. Applaud, witness, detach if she can, but not die.

Room 653 is bald too, clean-shaven after smashing into a windshield of a stolen car he careened into oncoming traffic. Both the men he hit died right there on the highway—a father driving his visiting son to the airport, a young and popular volleyball player, finishing his college career with 731 digs. His grinning picture was all over the news.

Even though the wreck was mid-afternoon, 653's blood toxicology screen was positive for methamphetamines, benzodiazepines, alcohol, and cocaine.

He's skinny. Street drugs suppressed his appetite's voice, tricking him into thinking he was not just high, but full. At first glance his body looks like it belongs to an emaciated, dying old man. Closer up it's easy to see his sculpted muscles are like hardwood. He's seventeen years old. He wears a plastic diaper, and his limbs are splayed like a book, his feet and hands tied to each corner of the bed so he doesn't hurt himself or us nurses. He yells nearly constantly. Most of the noises are unintelligible, but he does seem to know three words: *sit, no, how*. We're suspicious that *sit* is a mispronunciation. More often than not, *how* is a long sound with several syllables, like a chant. The emphasis is usually on the *ow*, leading us to wonder if he's in pain. We nurses give him analgesics even though the meds don't seem to do much. We give the meds because it makes us feel like we're doing something useful. We give them because his yelling drives us crazy.

He's a hard one to like, is 653. Most the time all we can do is retie him, put mitts on his hands so he doesn't chew into his own fingers or scratch himself bloody, clean him up from time to time. I've never seen anyone visit him, but there's a note on his board that says *Grandma and Noni love you. Get well soon.*

For someone tethered in four places, 653 is all over the bed. In just two weeks he's already rubbed his heels down to the bone. His diaper hangs low on his angled hips, and most of the time he's able to squirm out of it. If he gets his hands loose he tears up the diaper and eats it. Or throws punches. Last week he gave a night shift nurse a nasty bruise on her upper arm while she was pushing a syringe of liquid food into a gastric tube going into his abdomen. While her focus was on his G-tube, he bit through the wrist restraint and swung at an enemy none of the rest of us can see.

Teea is my age, and we've had a few good talks about God and destiny and health. Today, however, I spend my precious few extra moments here with 653. I don't really want to, but my job (as a pain and palliative care clinical nurse specialist) is to assess his discomfort. I also want to relieve the pain of the staff nurses, which will happen briefly if I can quiet him down.

His name is Brandon. I discovered yesterday that if I call him by name, he stops yelling. But when I start to leave he just starts up again, no matter how many tranquilizers or opiates the nurses give him.

"Brandon!" I shout over his shout. He makes full-on eye contact and stares like a baby does, not quite in focus but very intent on something he sees. Does he recognize his own name long enough to stop the spinning of some kaleidoscope of fears that dominate his visual field?

"Brandon, do you have pain?"

"No," he says, as clearly as if we'd just resumed a lucid conversation over a cup of coffee.

I take a couple of charts into his room. After I say his name and he goes silent, I do some paperwork. He stares at me, he stares at the walls, he stares into thin air. Every once in a while he tracks something across the ceiling, as if a shooting star has flared above him. His temporary quiet is a relief.

I tell him about things. Tonight I tell him I want to make a movie of him, to show high school kids what really happens on drugs. I figure the diaper might get them. I ask him how could it be that some people want to live with every fiber of their spirit and others seem to dare death to come get them. Brandon doesn't argue or interrupt. He lies there in total silence. He doesn't do it because he hears just any words, but because he hears a voice speak his name. His name is his talisman, his clue, his Geiger counter, his compass, his home base, his organizer, his horizon, his divining rod.

"Brandon, I have to go." He stares at my lips as if he hears something remotely familiar and unnerving, like the pulsing of a troubled mother's heart.

Heading toward Teea's room, I see her husband Robbie leaning against the wall outside her door. His eyes greet me with a grief as dense as the door itself and a question that has no answer. Still, his grief is soft somehow, a metal tempered with gratitude. Grief tempered by guilt is barbed wire.

I lean up against the wall next to him. He tells me that the hardest thing about Teea's diagnosis is the helplessness. A high school biology teacher, he likes tangibles. He tells me the ground beneath his feet moves like sand, he cannot find purchase.

Nooooooooooooo, shouts Brandon from 653.

I follow Robbie into Teea's room.

Honey, says Teea, seeing her husband's helplessness. Go sit with that young man next door, and Robbie leaves willingly, taking his question with him.

21

Message for Lent

Pope Francis

"Make your hearts firm."
—James 5:8

Dear Brothers and Sisters,

Lent is a time of renewal for the whole Church, for each community and every believer. Above all it is a "time of grace" (2 Cor 6:2). God does not ask of us anything that he himself has not first given us. "We love because he first has loved us" (1 Jn 4:19). He is not aloof from us. Each one of us has a place in his heart. He knows us by name, he cares for us, and he seeks us out whenever we turn away from him. He is interested in each of us; his love does not allow him to be indifferent to what happens to us. Usually, when we are healthy and comfortable, we forget about others (something God the Father never does): we are unconcerned with their problems, their sufferings and the injustices they endure . . . Our heart grows cold. As long as I am relatively healthy and comfortable, I don't think about those less well off. Today, this selfish attitude of indifference has taken on global proportions, to the extent that we can speak of a globalization of indifference. It is a problem which we, as Christians, need to confront.

When the people of God are converted to his love, they find answers to the questions that history continually raises. One of the most urgent challenges which I would like to address in this Message is precisely the globalization of indifference. Indifference to our neighbor and to God also represents a real temptation for us Christians. Each year during Lent we need to hear once more the voice of the prophets who cry out and trouble our conscience. God is not indifferent to our world; he so loves it that he gave his Son for our salvation. In the Incarnation, in the earthly life, death, and resurrection of the Son of God, the gate between God and man, between heaven and earth, opens once for all. The Church is like the hand holding open this gate, thanks to her proclamation of God's word, her celebration of the sacraments and her witness of the faith which works through love (cf. Gal 5:6). But the world tends to withdraw into itself and shut that door through which God comes into the world and the world comes to him. Hence the hand, which is the Church, must never be surprised if it is rejected, crushed and wounded. God's people, then, need this interior renewal, lest we become indifferent and withdraw into ourselves. To further this renewal, I would like to propose for our reflection three biblical texts.

1. "If one member suffers, all suffer together."
(1 Cor 12:26)—The Church

The love of God breaks through that fatal withdrawal into ourselves which is indifference. The Church offers us this love of God by her teaching and especially by her witness. But we can only bear witness to what we ourselves have experienced. Christians are those who let God clothe them with goodness and mercy, with Christ, so as to become, like Christ, servants of God and others. This is clearly seen in the liturgy of Holy Thursday, with its rite of the washing of feet. Peter did not want Jesus to wash his feet, but he came to realize that Jesus does not wish to be just an example of how we should wash one another's feet. Only those who have first allowed Jesus to wash their own feet can then offer this service to others. Only they have "a part" with him (Jn 13:8) and thus can serve others. Lent is a favorable time for letting Christ serve us so that we in turn may become more like him. This happens whenever we hear the word of God and receive the sacraments, especially the Eucharist. There we become what we receive: the Body of Christ. In this body there is no room for the indifference which so often seems to possess our hearts. For whoever is of Christ, belongs to one body, and in him we cannot be indifferent to one another. "If one part suffers, all the parts suffer with it; if one part is honored, all the parts share its joy" (1 Cor 12:26). The Church is the *communio sanctorum* not only because of her saints, but also because she is a communion in holy things: the love of God revealed to us in Christ and all his gifts. Among these gifts there is also the response of those who let themselves be touched by this love. In this communion of saints, in this sharing in holy things, no one possesses anything alone, but shares everything with others. And since we are united in God, we can do something for those who are far distant, those whom we could never reach on our own, because with them and for them, we ask God that all of us may be open to his plan of salvation.

2. "Where is your brother?"

(Gen4:9)—Parishes and Communities

All that we have been saying about the universal Church must now be applied to the life of our parishes and communities. Do these ecclesial structures enable us to experience being part of one body? A body which receives and shares what God wishes to give? A body which acknowledges and cares for its weakest, poorest and most insignificant members? Or do we take refuge in a universal love that would embrace the whole world, while failing to see the Lazarus sitting before our closed doors (Lk 16:19-31)? In order to receive what God gives us and to make it bear abundant fruit, we need to press beyond the boundaries of the visible Church in two ways. In the first place, by uniting ourselves in prayer with the Church in heaven. The prayers of the Church on earth establish a communion of mutual service and goodness which reaches up into the sight of God. Together with the saints who have found their fulfilment in God, we form part of that communion in which indifference is conquered by love. The Church in heaven is not triumphant because she has turned her back on the sufferings of the world and rejoices in splendid isolation. Rather, the saints already joyfully contemplate the fact that, through Jesus' death and resurrection, they have triumphed once and for all over indifference, hardness of heart and hatred. Until this victory of love penetrates the whole world, the saints continue to accompany us on our pilgrim way. Saint Therese of Lisieux, a Doctor of the Church, expressed her conviction that the joy in heaven for the victory of crucified love remains incomplete as long as there is still a single man or woman on earth who suffers and cries out in pain: "I trust fully that I shall not remain idle in heaven; my desire is to continue to work for the Church and for souls" (Letter 254, July 14, 1897). We share in the merits and joy of the saints, even as they share in our struggles and our longing for peace and reconciliation. Their joy in the victory of the Risen Christ gives us strength as we strive to overcome our indifference and hardness of heart.

In the second place, every Christian community is called to go out of itself and to be engaged in the life of the greater society of which it is a part, especially with the poor and those who are far away. The Church is missionary by her very nature; she is not self-enclosed but sent out to every nation and people. Her mission is to bear patient witness to the One who desires to draw all creation and every man and woman to the Father. Her mission is to bring to all a love which cannot remain silent. The Church follows Jesus Christ along the paths that lead to every man and woman, to the very ends of the earth (cf. Acts 1:8). In each of our neighbors, then, we must see a brother or sister for whom Christ died and rose again. What we ourselves have received, we have received for them as well. Similarly, all that our brothers and sisters possess is a gift for the Church and for all humanity.

Dear brothers and sisters, how greatly I desire that all those places where the Church is present, especially our parishes and our communities, may become islands of mercy in the midst of the sea of indifference!

3. "Make your hearts firm!"

(James 5:8)—Individual Christians

As individuals too, we are tempted by indifference. Flooded with news reports and troubling images of human suffering, we often feel our complete inability to help. What can we do to avoid being caught up in this spiral of distress and powerlessness? First, we can pray in communion with the Church on earth and in heaven. Let us not underestimate the power of so many voices united in prayer! The 24 Hours for the

Lord initiative, which I hope will be observed on 13-14 March throughout the Church, also at the diocesan level, is meant to be a sign of this need for prayer. Second, we can help by acts of charity, reaching out to both those near and far through the Church's many charitable organizations. Lent is a favorable time for showing this concern for others by small yet concrete signs of our belonging to the one human family. Third, the suffering of others is a call to conversion, since their need reminds me of the uncertainty of my own life and my dependence on God and my brothers and sisters. If we humbly implore God's grace and accept our own limitations, we will trust in the infinite possibilities which God's love holds out to us. We will also be able to resist the diabolical temptation of thinking that by our own efforts we can save the world and ourselves.

As a way of overcoming indifference and our pretensions to self-sufficiency, I would invite everyone to live this Lent as an opportunity for engaging in what Benedict XVI called a formation of the heart (cf. *Deus Caritas Est*, 31). A merciful heart does not mean a weak heart. Anyone who wishes to be merciful must have a strong and steadfast heart, closed to the tempter but open to God. A heart which lets itself be pierced by the Spirit so as to bring love along the roads that lead to our brothers and sisters. And, ultimately, a poor heart, one which realizes its own poverty and gives itself freely for others. During this Lent, then, brothers and sisters, let us all ask the Lord: *"Fac cor nostrum secundum cor tuum*: Make our hearts like yours"* (Litany of the Sacred Heart of Jesus). In this way we will receive a heart which is firm and merciful, attentive and generous, a heart which is not closed, indifferent or prey to the globalization of indifference. It is my prayerful hope that this Lent will prove spiritually fruitful for each believer and every ecclesial community. I ask all of you to pray for me. May the Lord bless you and Our Lady keep you.

~

22

Things Fall Apart

Peter Quinn

The greatest failure in America is the failure to stay young. It is a failure of imagination, the inability to grasp the alternatives offered by surgery, cosmetology, and pharmacology. It is a failure of will, the indiscipline that results in flagging energies, flabby bodies, and clogged arteries.

It is a failure of financial planning, the incapacity to amass the resources needed to deploy the full panoply of anti-aging techniques and technologies. Most basic of all, it is a failure of genetic foresight, the prenatal passivity that accepts a poisoned lineage of physical and mental infirmities, moral laxness, and hereditary balding.

For me, the nightfall of old age is particularly upsetting. I tried hard to seize and hold the day. I was born to healthy, middle-class parents in a good neighborhood. Except for college and that weekend in Las Vegas, I drank moderately. I exercised regularly and completed several marathons. I had regular checkups and took care of my teeth.

I've enjoyed a reasonably successful career, a happy marriage, and a retirement undimmed by fear of living in a cardboard box and subsisting on the kindness of strangers.

Some changes were only to be expected. At thirty, I faced up to male pattern baldness. At forty, I purchased my first pair of reading glasses. At fifty, I added Metamucil to my orange juice. At sixty, I started blood-pressure medication and did my best to eschew meat and order whatever fish was on the menu.

Despite hard work, sound planning, lifestyle adjustments, and unusually well-behaved Irish genes, I find myself—to paraphrase the poet Yeats—"where all the ladders" end, "in the foul rag and bone shop" of encroaching decrepitude.

One day I had hearing as good as a rabbit's. The next I suffered "sudden onset hearing loss." At cocktail parties, I can no longer distinguish conversation from background noise (not that it matters much). Going out to dinner requires several minutes of configuring the seating to compensate for my auditory deficiency.

I developed epilepsy. As a result, I can no longer drive, ride a bike, swim alone, or—not that I had ever had the desire—swing on a trapeze.

My knees resemble the coil springs on a rusted '56 Chevy. Two weeks ago, something snapped in my upper arm while doing my morning pushups. I can't lift my right arm above my shoulder. Last week, while jogging, I wrenched my back so badly I can't walk right. I had surgery for thyroid cancer. My medicine cabinet resembles the pickup window at the local pharmacy.

My powers of recall are showing signs of wear and tear. I open cabinets and drawers and instantly forget what I'm looking for. The ability to attach names to the faces of friends and acquaintances is becoming one of life's small triumphs.

"The wages of sin," wrote St. Paul, "is death." Either he forgot to mention or deliberately left out that so are the wages of virtue. We're all inching or hurtling toward the egress, and we Baby Boomers are elbowing our way to the head of the line. For us, keeping the Grim Reaper at bay looms as an increasingly expensive proposition.

It's true you can't take it with you. It's also true that we members of the over-sixty-five set will suck up a disproportionate share of the country's medical resources in order to make incremental additions to life spans already longer than those enjoyed by 99 percent of our ancestors.

The inevitability of the final curtain doesn't make it easier to accept. I'm as reluctant and fearful as anyone else to face the end. But, sooner or later, it's all right to think about making room instead of taking it up. A degree of resignation and acceptance isn't a bad thing.

We can claw and cry for a day or two more and spend whatever it takes. We can rage against the dying of the light and resent it as a violation of an imagined right to live forever. Or we can enjoy what we're still capable of enjoying and exit, if not laughing, then with a smile of gratitude for the miracle of existence we've been privileged to share.

🖋

23

A Rose by Any Other Name

James T. Keane

Everyone named Jim Keane is a bumbling ne'er-do-well.

You may have examples to the contrary, but I have known them all already, known them all: the Jim Keane in Finland who stole his brother's plumbing tools; the homonymous wanker in Liverpool who never paid his mother back for the pounds she laid out for his soccer tickets; the salesman traveling internationally who made his driver sleep under his bed because he didn't want to pay for a second hotel room; the backpacker in Europe who's sleeping his way across the continent; the hipster in San Francisco who asked his sister to cover his security deposit and now wants her to collect payment from their parents; the Jim Keane in Ireland who responds to every entreaty that he reconcile with his family with the line "don't put a candle on a turd and call it a birthday cake, because I just won't eat it"; and, alas, many, many more.

I don't know any of these people personally, mind you, but I have read plenty about them. When I think of all of us as a composite, I imagine something like the Ronnie Dobbs of *Mr. Show* fame, somehow at the center of trouble in every corner of the globe, always ready with an excuse, and very rarely up to any good. It's a source of a great deal of name shame, and I'm hardly off the hook myself; I have a friend named Jim Keene who has suffered mightily over the years reading emails meant for me, some of which surely made him want to wash his eyes out with bleach. Just one more missive to one more Jim Keane, explaining that, well, mistakes were made!

And just how, exactly, do I have access to the grimy details of the lives of my fellow Jims, you ask? Among the trades I have plied over the years was as an .html programmer for a dotcom back in the 1990s. It was the era when free web-based email became available for the first time, and I was more or less at the front of the line since I spent my entire working day on the Internet, and so I got a variation on my name that was simple and direct. I still use that email address, though nowadays it serves mostly as a backup for an address much more recherché.

So let's say you're angry with the Jim Keane in your life (it happens). You shoot off an impassioned email but don't necessarily check to see if you got his address perfectly right, or maybe you don't know his exact email address, or maybe he LIED TO YOU and gave you a fake email address to buy himself some time. In more cases than you'd think, you've sent that furious email to me by mistake, and over the past fifteen years I've seen some real doozies. The sad truth is that I never know how to respond.

"Wrong Jim, sorry for your troubles"?

"Consider the beam in thine own eye"?

"You and me both, sister"?

Ignoring them is not an option—Jim Keanes all over the world use this as an avoidance strategy, so usually the sender is hip to that game. I used to let them know they had the wrong guy, until one interlocutor (with, awkwardly, the same name as my sister) told me off for reading her private correspondence. What was I supposed to do? It was sent to me with a subject heading that read, "Wait until you hear what Dad said this time." Curiosity kills this cat!

In any case, one would think that it would be impossibly annoying to be mistaken repeatedly for someone else with the same name, particularly when it seems the only decent fellows who share your name are a few firemen and cops (come to think of it, the one Jim Keane who had been seen exiting a subway car in Brooklyn when he was supposed to be visiting his mother in Brookline actually WAS a fireman). And I'm hardly going to pretend that I haven't been horrified and dismayed at some of the shenanigans we Jim Keanes manage to pull off, or some of our excuses for how those shenanigans came to pass. Over time, however, something curious has happened with these emails (they still come; I got one just a few weeks ago); I began to find them endearing. Most of these fellows, after all, weren't necessarily all bad. They just seemed to make the wrong choices at the wrong times, and had an alarming (and sometimes hilarious) propensity for saying the wrong thing when trying to explain themselves. Their foibles were rarely on the level of anything really evil or dastardly—they ran into trouble with money, with sex, with family dynamics, with taking responsibility for their own actions. But are those such unfamiliar stories to the rest of us?

Another point: If you look closely enough at any human drama, you discover that no situation is as black and white as the text it's presented on. A lot of my fellow Jim Keanes are on the run from something, but some of them are on the run from *someone*—and with good reason. For example, the aforementioned backpacker with the roving eye? His girlfriend had cheated on him, but was trying to track him down somewhere in Europe. Why? She wanted him to know (even though she had ditched him for some Italian lothario she met on their travels) that, "I am still your booshie and you're my pookie even if we're not together anymore." Booshie? Pookie? Her I really wanted to write back, because I had a few things to say.

The familiarity of such tales of human woe and sin and confusion, especially during a season of penitence and repentance such as Lent, gets to the heart of a human reality that isn't always easy to put into words, but which a former professor of mine, a priest, laid out succinctly when discussing what it's like to hear confessions. "Sooner or later," he said, "every single one of us finds him- or herself in a grimy roadhouse on the roadside of life. And none of us are quite sure how we got there." That same professor said something else: that the primary experience of every confessor is not how evil people are, but how good they are—how inspiring it can be to see people trying hard to do the right thing, how remorseful people can be for the mistakes they make, how much they desire reconciliation with God and with each other in lives that are complicated, messy, encumbered by sin in ways that they can and can't control. Rare indeed is the person whose sinfulness or stupidity is not even more vexing for him or herself than it is for the people whom he or she has hurt.

Of course, it may be true that the people who need a Lent before Easter tend to be a self-selecting sample. Maybe there are many of us human beings who are truly impenitent and feel no need for forgiveness. Or maybe, just maybe, a lot of us are afraid to ask for it.

In any case, there's a valuable Lenten lesson for all of us when we see the foibles of our peers laid out in such stark detail, a lesson that perhaps we've already learned but could still stand some repetition: there is nothing new under the sun, and there's usually not that much difference between the best of us and the ne'er-do-wells among us. We all need and want reconciliation at some level or another, and most of us know it about ourselves before we know it about someone else.

Deep down in our hearts, most of us want to pay for the pilfered plumbing kit, apologize to the slighted friend, and to make right with God and with each other what went wrong in a thousand and one ways in our lives. And, God knows, we're all a little closer to holiness than we, our namesakes, our peers, or even those who stand in judgment over us might think.

🌿

24

Eastering Joy

Joyce Rupp

"You will weep and mourn, while the world rejoices;
you will grieve, but your grief will become joy."
—Jn 16:20

These consoling words of Jesus in John's Gospel frequently call me to an awareness of the human condition when I come to church on Easter Sunday morning. As I enter the hallowed space, I look around at the great variety of people gathered for a liturgy richly strewn with alleluias. As the crowd streams into the pews, a number of the congregation reveal an easy happiness, noticeably ready to revel in Easter's rejoicing. Others, it seems to me, might not be so easily moved to express that spirit of joy.

While "Hello" and "Happy Easter" circle in the

air, I wonder about those present who are having difficulty sensing the emotion of gladness prominently emphasized in the feast. External displays of lilies and other bright flowers, colorful dress and pleasant greetings do not necessarily reflect the inner life of all of those who have come to worship. There are persons who step inside the church bringing a "weeping and mourning" spirit with them, still waiting for their "grief" to transform into the joy promised by Jesus.

It doesn't take long to find evidence of the lack of joy. In the gathering I notice widows in their isolated loneliness, bored teenagers with eyes secreted on digital devices, weary adults with dull expressions, disabled elderly stooped with physical pain, and numerous persons who show evidence of the stress and anxiety due to life's rapid pace and unexpected hardships.

When I observe this diversity of emotions, I question if those without much joy expect to receive a heart of jubilation at the liturgy. More likely they come with tattered bits of doubt, regret or guilt, thinking they *ought* to feel joyful instead of how they actually feel— tense, wearied, downhearted, distracted, pained, and lacking a felt sense of spiritual connection to the day's message of jubilation.

These worshipers are not alone in carrying more

glumness than cheerfulness. As lectors proclaim the scriptures for the day, those of us in the pews hear anew how the disciples were lost in caverns of their own disappointment and vanished hope. These friends of the Risen Christ most surely did not have alleluias in their hearts immediately following the execution of their beloved friend. They, too, had to have joy coaxed out of them. The presence of the Risen One slowly drew this gift forth. Similarly, the scriptures, prayers and songs of the Easter liturgy can serve to begin releasing the buried joy within the downhearted.

Because of the less-than-joyful emotional response existing within some of those present at the Easter liturgies, I offer the following prayer. May it be helpful for any of us when we enter the season of the Resurrection with our inner world crying out for the joy of the Risen One.

• • •

Risen Jesus, assure me of your promised joy.

Reenergize whatever in my spirit has crept into the cave of gloom. Bring it forth into the light of your radiance.

Reestablish attentiveness to the joy found in nature's continual unfolding of the seasons, each one with its own inherent beauty.

Reinvigorate a desire to enter each day confident of your grace to help sustain a positive perspective, no matter what the perils or distress confronting me.

Renew an ability to find satisfaction in my faith without having to poke continually at truths that remains hidden.

Resist my attempts to foster complete control and thus miss the joy of risk-taking, adventure and the call to step out of my tightly bound securities.

Reclaim love grown cold or dormant due to neglect, misperception, or the deluge of overwork that quickly steals affection from my heart.

Restore order and balance in my mind. Clear it of tangling thoughts, judgments, and issues that stealthily poison an enjoyment of life.

Resurrect the undivided passion I once had for bringing the best of my inner goodness to each and every part of all I am and all I do.

Reveal what keeps playfulness from emerging and forfeits the freedom to express the laughter hiding inside of me.

Release the door of my heart to enter the tender moments, the happy events and the unforeseen experiences holding great joy if only I am open to them.

Creator of Joy, lift out of my heart any heaviness

or doldrums residing there. Turn my attention toward daily opportunities to rejoice: the colors, shapes and sounds of beauty my eyes and ears unconsciously see and hear, unexpected kindness, the dawning of each new day, the quiet approaching of night, and all those little lifts of joy I can quickly pass by without noticing or offering thanks. Reach me with your Eastering joy and tuck me happily into your ever-present gladness. Amen.

25

𝒦

Two Old People and a Young Man with a Gun

Jim Forest

This is a story that I've told before and will probably tell again. It has to do with an elderly couple and a young man with a gun. It's a story of protecting the life of an enemy by treating him as a welcome guest and, in the process, perhaps saving several lives, including their own. It's a story that demonstrates the truth of an insight of Saint John of the Cross: "Where there is no love, put love, and you will find love."

Louise and Nathan Degrafinried, both in their seventies at the time, lived in Mason, Tennessee. They were members of the Mount Sinai Primitive Baptist Church.

One morning in February 1984, Riley Arzeneaux,

a man who escaped from the state prison several days earlier, came into their house. He aimed a shotgun at Louise and Nathan and shouted, "Don't make me kill you!"

Louise responded to this nightmarish event as calmly as a grandmother normally responds to the crises and accidents that befall a grandchild. "Young man," she said, "I am a Christian lady. I don't believe in violence. Put down that gun and you sit down. I don't allow no violence here." Riley obediently put the weapon on the couch. He said, "Lady, I'm hungry. I haven't eaten in three days."

While Nathan got their unexpected guest a pair of dry socks, Louise made a substantial breakfast: bacon and eggs, toast, milk, and coffee. She put out their best napkins.

When the three of them sat down to eat, she took Riley's hand in her own and said, "Young man, let's give thanks that you came here and that you are safe." She said a prayer and asked him if there was anything he would like to say to the Lord. He couldn't think of anything so she suggested, "Just say, 'Jesus wept.'" (A journalist later asked how she happened to choose that text. Louise replied, "Because I figured that he didn't have no church background, so I wanted to start him off simple; something short, you know.")

After breakfast she held Riley's hand again. He was trembling all over. "Young man, I love you and God loves you. God loves all of us, every one of us, especially you. Jesus died for you because he loves you so much."

Then the police arrived. Hearing the approaching sirens, Riley said, "They gonna kill me when they get here." But Louise said she was going out to talk to them. Standing on her porch, she spoke to the police in the same terms she had spoken to the convict: "Y'all put those guns away. I don't allow no violence here."

The police, as docile in their response to Louise as Riley had been, put their guns back in their holsters. Soon afterward, Riley was taken back to the prison. No one was harmed.

Louise and Nathan Degrafinried might also have been killed, of course. Good, decent people die tragically every day. But actually it isn't so surprising that their warm welcome to a frightened man provided them with more security than any gun.

The story does not end with Riley's return to prison. Louise and Nathan were asked to press charges against him for holding them hostage but declined to do so. "That boy did us no harm," Louise insisted. As both she and Nathan refused to testify, the charges were dropped, though his prison sentence was extended for having escaped. Louise initiated correspondence with Riley. She asked for his photo and put it in her family album. Throughout his remaining years in prison—Riley was freed in 1995—Louise kept in touch with Riley and he with her. Louise actively worked for Riley's release. "He usually called on her birthday and around Christmastime," Louise's daughter, Ida Marshall, related to a reporter after her mother's death in 1998.

Louise had an enormous impact on Riley's life. "After looking back over all my life in solitary, I realized I'd been throwing my life away," he said in a 1991 interview. Riley recalls praying with Louise Degrafinried when she came to visit him in prison. "She started off her prayer," he recalled, "by saying, 'God, this is your child. You know me, and I know you.'" "That's the kind of relationship I want to have with God," Riley said. In 1988, Riley became a Christian. "I realized," he explained, "that meeting the Degrafinrieds and other things that happened in my life just couldn't be coincidences. After all that, I realized someone was looking over me."

Louise Degrafinried was often asked about the day she was held hostage. "Weren't you terrified?" a reporter wondered. "I wasn't alone," she responded. "My Savior was with me, and I was not afraid."

It's similar to a comment Riley made when explaining the events that led to his conversion. "Mrs. Degrafinried was real Christianity," he told mourners at her funeral. "No fear." Riley sat with immediate family in the front pew at the service and was among those carrying Louise Degrafinried's coffin to its burial place.

Louise and Nathan have died, but the story of their welcoming an escaped convict has become a parable of hospitality and the works of mercy: "I was on the run and you took me in, I was hungry and you made me breakfast, I was thirsty and you gave me coffee, I had wet socks on my feet and you gave me dry ones, I was ready to kill and you freed me from my weapon."

🖎

26

The River

Paul Myers

Many years ago I was fishing in the Wilson River with my brother-in-law. It was autumn, salmon season. The air and the river were cold and you could smell the sea. Yellow and gold and bronze leaves darted and swirled and spun in the crystalline waters at our feet. Morning mist hung in the hemlocks and firs climbing the mountains. Everywhere there was mottled light.

I heard the sound of plastic hitting rock and I looked over and saw my brother-in-law lean over to retrieve his lure box from the river, and then he slipped and fell in, and the river yanked him away. He groped frantically for the rocks and jabbed his heels desperately into the riverbed and after a second or two he actually stood up, the pounding water fanning out behind him high and wide as a peacock's tail; and then the river grabbed him and pulled him straight down into its bosom and he vanished.

I dropped my gear and ran as fast as my waders would allow, ducking and shoving through alder and vine maple and devil's club, and I clambered up on the boulder where he had been seconds ago but there was nothing in the river but his hat.

I screamed his name again and again and again and again and again. His hat whipped away down the river.

Please God help please God

I read that water desperately, anything, a ripple of him, any hint of his life, any hint of his body, his color, his face.

Please God please

I don't know how much time went by, a minute, two minutes, and then I noticed a thick tree branch jammed in the backwater at the head of the gorge. A sparrow lit on a ledge above the branch and then launched upriver just inches over the riffles. The branch rolled a bit and I realized it was his leg, and I screamed his name, I screamed and screamed, but his head was underwater, and he was dead.

Please God help me

I ran downstream to the footbridge and ran across and climbed down to a dozen feet above him and yelled and pleaded. I went a little mad maybe. I wanted to throw rocks and sticks at him, pry him loose, throw some of my life at him and into him.

Please God

I ran up to the highway and waited forever with my heart pounding. There was a moment when I felt, with every fiber of my being, that his spirit, his soul, was rising out of the canyon. I cannot describe how sacred that moment was, how absolutely sure his soul was departing his body and rising up over the waters.

He was the happiest man alive, my brother-in-law. He had said so hours before. He and his wife were expecting their first child in two months. They had just purchased their first house. He had finally landed his dream job. His beloved college football team was going to the Rose Bowl. He was going to fish for salmon with new fishing gear that he had waited years to afford. He was beaming.

A water ouzel landed a few inches from his body and jumped back and forth into the river, catching breakfast.

Cars stopped. Finally there were eight men. Some had been fishing for salmon at the coast. Some had been crabbing in the bay. One was a New York City fireman on vacation.

We went to get the body. The fireman tied a rope around his own body. We lowered him down to the body. We dug our feet into the sand and gravel for leverage and hauled the fireman and my brother-in-law out of the river. By now search and rescue teams and emergency medical technicians and the deputy sheriff were there. They cut his boots off and tried to resuscitate him but he was dead.

We carried him up the steep uneven trail to the highway. An ambulance roared thirty minutes to the nearest hospital. I could not speak. A doctor pronounced him officially dead. I was led into a chapel. A minister came and sat with me and we prayed aloud. I wept and wept and wept until I was exhausted.

I cannot articulate how much pain I have felt and seen in the fourteen years since I saw my brother-in-law die in front of me. I loved that man, and I weep over the scars his sudden death caused his wife and child and clan. I cannot articulate the dark swirl of emotions and feelings and agonies in me since that moment. I cannot explain how hard I have tried to live up to the kind and generous and compassionate words people have said to me about his sudden death, my utter helplessness. I cannot explain how many thousands of hours I have asked God why my brother-in-law was taken so tragically, why I was chosen to witness such a horror.

I have never written about his death before, and I struggle to do so now; but after years of struggling and healing and praying, I tell you my story. I was witness to a moment of incredible holiness, and I can no longer lock that up inside of my heart. I saw a man's soul leave his first temple and rise toward his next temple. I saw him depart from this planet.

I will see his face and hear his voice again, and that will be a joy I cannot understand. But I know that it will come.

~ ✍ ~

27

It Is in Pardoning that We Are Pardoned

Leonardo Boff

One of the most surprising and even scandalous dimensions of the message of Jesus is the proclamation that his God is a God of unconditional love and unlimited mercy. He offers his love and forgiveness to all, even when that love is not returned. He loves even the "ungrateful and evil" (Lk 6:35).

Such good news left the pious of his own time puzzled and still causes confusion today among people who strive to obey the commandments and make themselves pleasing to God. How can God also love the impious, sinners, exploiters, and evildoers? This is the paradox of Jesus' revolutionary message: God goes after the sheep that has gone astray and searches for the lost coin, runs out to meet the prodigal son and rejoices more over the sinner who repents than over the ninety-nine just who are saved. Jesus says, "I have not come to call the just, but sinners" (Mk 2:17). How can we fail to be surprised at such words?

Curiously, all of Jesus' parables about forgiveness and mercy are aimed at the hardness of heart of pious persons of his time. The parables of the Pharisee and the publican (Lk 18:9-14) and the prodigal son (Lk 15:11-32) seek to show that in order to please God, besides being faithful and good, we must also be merciful and wish to forgive, to forgive "seventy times seven" (Mt 18:22), that is, without limit. We must seek "to be merciful just as your Father is merciful" (Lk 6:36).

If God forgives us so unreservedly, how can we not also forgive those who offend us? The gospel is emphatic: "For if you forgive others their transgressions, your heavenly Father will also forgive you; but if you do not forgive others, neither will your Father forgive your transgressions" (Mt 6:14-15). Is this some kind of negotiation with God? No. It has to do with understanding that "the measure with which you measure will be measured out to you" (Mt 7:2). According to the parable, the indebted servant was completely forgiven for the thousands of denarii that he owed, but he did not forgive his fellow servant who owed him a few coins. The master called him and told him, "You wicked slave! I forgave you all that debt because you pleaded with me. Should you not have had mercy on your fellow slave, as I had mercy on you?" (Mt 18:32-33). The lesson is crystal clear: "Just as the Lord has forgiven you, so you also must forgive" (Col 3:13).

This attitude is not easy for those whose sense of justice is merely human. Do not many say "I'd rather die than forgive"? We must live the experience of being radically forgiven in our offenses to feel impelled to forgive without reservations and with a free heart.

At the culmination of history, works of mercy will count. They will enable the supreme and merciful Judge to announce: "Come, you who are blessed by my Father, inherit the kingdom prepared for you from the foundation of the world" (Mt 25:34).

What does it mean existentially to forgive? It means seeking to go beyond oneself, leaving bitterness and the will to vengeance behind, and reaching a higher level from which we will be able to see differently the one who has done injury. Such people are not simply people who have done wrong. They are an infinite openness, children of God, and brothers and sisters in our shared humanity. Hence, they cannot be reduced to simply being "offenders" and "sinners." Forgiving means preventing them from being held hostage to the consequences of the wrongful acts they have committed. Forgiving means the ability to support and maintain the bond of communion even when the other side is closed and the other margin disappears. It means allowing love to flow once more. Wagering on this positive side means creating through forgiveness the conditions for a relationship of shared life in kinship.

🖎

28

Spring

Mary Oliver

Somewhere
    a black bear
        has just risen from sleep
            and is staring

down the mountain.
    All night
        in the brisk and shallow restlessness
            of early spring

I think of her,
    her four black fists
        flicking the gravel,
            her tongue

like a red fire
    touching the grass,
        the cold water.
            There is only one question:

how to love this world.
    I think of her
        rising
            like a black and leafy ledge

to sharpen her claws against
    the silence
        of the trees.
            Whatever else

my life is
    with its poems
        and its music
            and its glass cities,

it is also this dazzling darkness
    coming
        down the mountain,
            breathing and tasting;

All Shall Be Well

all day I think of her—
    her white teeth,
        her wordlessness,
            her perfect love.

🖎

29

The Father of Mercies

Matt Malone, SJ

The fire radio woke my father from a well-deserved sleep and notified him of a car accident that had just occurred a quarter-mile from our home on Cape Cod. He was accustomed to being awakened by emergencies. This sort of night was familiar to him as a veteran firefighter: the adrenaline kick-start, the frantic search for his shoes, the flight to the scene. Dad was the first to arrive, several minutes before the ambulance. He found an overturned car and a driver who was confused but conscious. Quickly moving to the passenger's side of the vehicle, he assessed the condition of the unconscious victim still trapped inside. From his years of experience he knew immediately that the injuries would be fatal. There was nothing in his experience, however, that prepared him for a more horrifying discovery: the victim was his son.

After what seemed like a lifetime for my father, the ambulance crew arrived, freed my brother from the car and transported him to the nearby hospital. A death watch followed. When it was clear that Joe was brain dead, my father ordered the removal of advanced life support and Joe died a few hours later, on July 31, 1984, the feast of St. Ignatius Loyola. He was sixteen years old. The driver of the vehicle, my brother's seventeen-year-old friend Kenny, was treated for minor injuries and released. Soon afterward, he was cited for six criminal infractions in connection with the accident, including vehicular homicide because he was driving under the influence of alcohol.

The following November, Kenny pleaded guilty to the charges and was awaiting sentencing. Under the Victim/Witness Act that had just been passed in Massachusetts, my father was invited to submit a statement about the impact of the event on him and his family that could be taken into consideration by the judge. Dad said that he would do so and asked to deliver it in person.

On the day of the sentencing, Dad rose and faced the judge and in a quavering voice told the court that the days between the accident—a scene "permanently etched" in his mind—and Joe's inevitable death marked "the most horrible week of my life." He continued:

> My son Joseph was a bright, good-natured young man with enormous potential. The emotional impact of this event on my family has been devastating. Today the driver of the vehicle stands before you awaiting sentencing. He has admitted to his guilt. He was Joseph's friend and co-worker; yet through the thoughtlessness of his actions, Joseph is dead. Kenny didn't approach that terrible night with the thought of harming anyone, least of all his friend, but the result is that one young man is dead, our family has suffered, his family has suffered, and not least of all, he himself has suffered. Kenny has to bear the knowledge of what he did for the rest of his life. That burden is far greater than any punishment this court could dispense. For this reason, I respectfully request that this court hear the appeal of the victim's parents and family and impose the minimum possible sentence.

The judge granted my father's request. Kenny received a six-month suspended jail sentence and two years of probation and was ordered to perform one thousand hours of community service.

In the twenty years since Joe's death, especially in these years of preparation for priestly ordination, I have often reflected on my father's extraordinary action. It seems all the more extraordinary, because my dad is what most people would call an ordinary man. "I just did what I thought was right," was how he recently spoke of it. But in doing what he "thought was right," my father performed the most powerful act of Christian charity I have ever personally witnessed. Of course he would never describe it that way, but I do, because I see in it much of what Jesus meant when he spoke of forgiveness.

How was Dad able to forgive Kenny? How was Jesus able to forgive the woman at the well or the woman caught in adultery? I suspect that my father saw in Kenny what Jesus saw in the women: their humanity. Kenny was fully human in my father's eyes. When Dad looked at Kenny, he of course saw the man who had killed his son, but he saw much more than that. He saw a kid who had killed his friend, a good kid who had made a tragic mistake. If all that Kenny was to my Dad was Joe's killer, there would have been no hope. But my father was somehow able to see a hope-filled future, Kenny's future, somewhere beyond the painful present. Kenny's mistake was not all that he was or could become. In my father's eyes, Joe's death was Kenny's doing, but it was not his being.

I suspect that the forgiveness Jesus asks of us begins with our seeing the ones who have harmed us in this same way, as fully human. Rabbi Harold Kushner has written that faith gives us "eyes with which to see the world." Our Christian vocation is to see the world in exactly that way. Through the eyes of faith, we can faintly see our fellow human beings, even and especially those who have sinned against us, as God sees them. We can begin to understand that the totality of someone's doings, however ferocious they may be, is never the total of someone's being. We may still be hurt, afraid and angry. The feelings may linger for a lifetime. No matter how hurt, afraid or angry we are, no human being is ever a monster. We may find it difficult to love, but through the eyes of faith we can begin to see that every man and woman is always and everywhere loved as much by God as are our greatest saints. That love alone is worthy of our greatest efforts to understand and to forgive.

The world is desperate for the radical forgiveness of which Jesus spoke and my father offered Kenny. The Catholic theologian James Alison offers a helpful image in his exegesis of the biblical story of Jonah. Sometimes, he says, it is as if we are on a ship in a storm, tossed by the tempest, struggling to find our way. The passengers are frightened; some think the best way to calm the storm is to find someone they can sacrifice to the angry God. How many times do we hear people blame "them"—whoever "they" happen to be. We scurry about the deck, looking for an "other," a Jonah we can toss overboard.

In the midst of his storm, my father could have made Kenny his Jonah, his "other," but he didn't. In addition to simply doing what he "thought was right," I suspect that my Dad also knew that tossing Kenny overboard would not calm the storm inside; it would not take away the memory of that terrible night. My father knew that somehow his own healing was to be found in his act of forgiveness. In a way, Kenny's destiny was his own: "We, though many, are one body in Christ and individually one of another" (Rom 12:5).

In the years after the accident, Kenny struggled, but he survived. He left Cape Cod and now lives a quiet life with his wife and two children in a town just outside Boston. He has written to my father faithfully for twenty years. My father does not share these letters with us. But he does like to make a point now and then of telling us that Kenny is doing okay and that he has made something of his life. Perhaps there's a bit of pride in that, but I doubt it. More likely it is relief that some life has come from such a terrible death.

In a few years, I hope to be ordained a priest. As a priest, I will be privileged to hear the struggles of ordinary people during the sacrament of reconciliation. I will listen attentively, offer some words of counsel and then pronounce the words, "God, the Father of mercies, through the death and resurrection of his Son, has reconciled the world to himself and sent the Holy Spirit among us for the forgiveness of sins. . . ." In that moment, I will also recall another father who, through the death of his son, forgave the seemingly unforgivable, allowing a shaft of light to pierce the darkness of a weary world.

30

Reading the Gospels

Jean Vanier

August 1997, Orval Monastery

Dear Friends,

This last year Jesus has led me more deeply into John's Gospel. I always feel the need to be in direct contact with Scripture, the Word of God, the words of Jesus. . . . It is as if John is taking me by the hand and leading me into a deeper union with Jesus in order to discover more totally his message of love. Let me explain.

After the prologue, John's Gospel begins as John the Baptist points to Jesus, calling him the "Lamb of God," not a powerful leader or a strutting general or a politician seeking acclaim and votes, but a lamb. This gentle lamb attracts two of John the Baptist's disciples, Andrew and (most probably) John, who start to follow him. Jesus turns to them and asks, "What are you looking for?" They reply, "Where do you live?" They want to be with him, to sit at his feet and learn from him. "Come and see," says Jesus.

Then Jesus attracts or calls his first followers. Over a short period of only two or three years, he forms and transforms their hearts, their inner attitudes and motivations.

Do you know where he brings them first of all? To a wedding feast in Cana! Why? Because "the kingdom of God is like a wedding feast." A wedding is a sign of love, unity, peace, fecundity, where a man and a woman become one flesh. We are not all called to be married, but we are all called to the wedding feast of the Lamb as described in the book of Revelation. The celebration in Cana, however, is not an ordinary wedding. It is a celebration where water will be changed into wine. Our humanity is called to be transformed by God, our hearts of stone into hearts of flesh, so that the ecstasy of life, light, and love becomes ours.

Then Jesus reveals to his disciples that he is the new temple where God resides; his body is now the place of love, of forgiveness, of communion, from which all life and love flow. Then Nicodemus is shown to us, and with him Jesus reveals that the ultimate gift of ecstasy, of total fulfillment for each one of us, comes only as we are born anew, from above, transformed by water and the Spirit.

After that Jesus does not lead his followers to a school of learning but to people in pain. He reveals to them the compassion in his own heart toward the poor, the broken, the oppressed, and how he comes to bring them life and hope: good news. He takes them first to a poor woman, of another religion and ethnic group, a woman of ill repute, who is alone and lonely and who feels guilty; she has lived already with five different men. Then they meet a poor father, crushed by pain; his little boy is dying. Then they go to the local psychiatric hospital or asylum, the pool of Bethesda, where "there were crowds of sick people: blind, lame, and paralyzed." I myself have visited many such places in our world; they are the places where all the unwanted are dumped. I am touched that this is one of the first places Jesus brings his disciples to, so that they may meet people who are broken, rejected, and in pain, and discover how he sees them, is close to them and loves them. Then the disciples begin to experience their own hearts opening up in compassion.

~

31

Near Journey's End

Howard Thurman

The disintegration of human life is always difficult to handle emotionally. The wasting away in illness, the gradual fading of one's intellectual powers, the quiet ebbing of physical energy, all these are part of the disintegration of human life, with which we have to do. One watches the appearance of the first strand of gray in the hair and then, quickly or creepily, the hair blossoms with heavy frost; or the first signs of baldness, and then more and more, until one's face extends up beyond the horizon to find fulfillment in a hairy fringe on the back of the head just above the neckline; or the first crow's feet around the eyes, and then here and there a wrinkle, and then more and more, until at last the fact of ripeness of years or premature physical cracking must be dealt with fully. At such times we are apt to feel as if life is taking unfair advantage of us, stripping us of all defenses of self-respect against the world. As we watch our own powers fade, or those of our friends, we wish that life were not so tenacious. Why can we not make a clean break of life without wasting away? It is humiliating.

When such thoughts crowd into one's mind, it is good to remember that it is precisely the tenacity of life, the way in which life squeezes each solitary bit of energy out of every available source, that has made survival possible and the endurance of the "slings of outrageous fortune" within the range of the creative powers of the human spirit. Man is tough! Man's body is tough! Man's mind is tough! Again and again, the story is that man crumbles rather than crashes. (For the first time in our history, the tempo of life is so heightened that there may not be time enough to crumble, only to crash.) Life is alive, and every tiny rootlet and every tiny nerve cell charged with the energy of the eternal. Old age, sickness, the fading of the powers is fought inch by inch all the way to the grave. Hallelujah!

❦

32

The Face of Christ

Daniel Berrigan, SJ

Some years ago I stood on an ancient outpost of western Ireland, off County Mayo. It was an island named
Caher, or "Saints' Island." Preserved there are several
quite remarkable relics, including a monastic ruin, cir-
cumscribing an altar of stones.

And scattered across the modest hills like a procession is a series of standing stones. These stones
invited attentiveness as I made my way across the
green land. The thin slabs, I was told, had been carved
by monks and set in place, fronting the harsh climate
of the northern seas.

And there the stones stood and withstood for
some fourteen centuries.

Each stone is incised with a different symbol; some

of great simplicity, others more cunningly carved; runes, Celtic curlicues, spirals interlaced, even a fish or bird. The tallest of the stones is not very tall, a matter of five feet or so. But it stops one in his tracks. For it bears a curious emblem, different from all the rest. A small medallion, perhaps five inches in diameter— a human face amid all the symbols.

The face of Christ. The first face of Christ, I was told, in Europe. A momentous breakthrough indeed. For the previous five centuries, images of Christ were symbolic, borrowed from nonhuman creation—cross forms, pelicans, dolphins, elegant or rude, carved or painted or set in mosaic.

One wonders why the literal image was so tardy in arriving. Was Christ's humanity too problematic? Or was the manner of his death—excruciating, disgraceful, a capital execution—beyond bearing in permanent form?

Whatever the cause, generations of Christian artists turned to symbols, groping toward, even while distancing from, our central mystery.

One speculates that during those centuries, a question was hovering in the air, gathering force. Granted that the Gospels offered no physical description of the Savior, it remained true that in Christ, God wore a human face. And what was the art, the faith, the community to make of that? Was the accessible Incarnate One to remain inaccessible to art—or accessible only through hints and emblems?

On Saints' Island, a literal finisterre, a land's end which must be thought of also as a new beginning, a source—a handful of anonymous monks took tools in hand. Christ inaccessible? From the promontory they cut and hauled a slab of stone. Then they incised an image both momentous and modest—the face of Christ, the art of Europe.

In regard to this event, I may have heard a memory drawn from folklore rather than from literal fact. There may have existed other, even older images of Christ, of which we know nothing, they having crumbled or been destroyed.

All this may be true, but I find it of small interest. The standing stones of Saints' Island beckon one, not to speculation or art history, but to pondering, to a deep heartfelt pause of breath, to a center all but lost. On a little wind-scoured, uninhabited island, one may for a time cast off the folly and fury, the anomie and despair of the Western adventure in the world.

The power of the place, the images, the trajectory of ruins and crosses! A place of healing, inevitably. To the island each summer comes an aquatic procession of the ill, brought there in curraghs, to touch the ruined altar called the Bed of Saint Patrick.

It was midwinter when we landed, a friend and I. The winds blew and blew, merciless, cleansing. It seemed to me, as I moved about like a sleepwalker, that I and those I love, who stand perilously near the end of things, stood for a time at a place where beginnings are, where new beginnings may yet be possible.

For an hour or so I wandered among the sentinel stones. Then I stood for a long time facing the face of Christ. And I thought of the fate of that crude and astonishing image, how it was multiplied, modified, stolen and borrowed, conjured and defiled, again and again in the hearts and guts and hands of Christians.

Artists and saints and martyrs seized the image for their own. So did scoundrels and conquistadors. Century after century, sometimes secretly and under threat of law, sometimes in rich processions, they bore the image across borders and continents, invoked its power upon causes shameful and holy, upon wars and crusades and pogroms, upon plagues and catastrophes in nature.

In the image of that image, what crimes and follies, what astonishing heroism, what poetry, what visions! They summoned the face in heroic witness, in courts and prisons and places of execution.

Thus the powers of this world, as well as the powerless, seized on this modest icon. Our own, our own! Uprooted from monkish soil, set like a stone sail in a preternatural barque, blown by winds of time far from its planting—the image became the common property and possession of humankind, transformed mightily, jealously. A terrible beauty was born.

Thus we have had, in turn upon bloody turn, the Christ of bosses and barons, of thieves and diplomats and generals, of entrepreneurs and oligarchs. And finally in our own lifetime, a Christ of Armageddon, itching for showdown. A Christ who saves some, we are told, by destroying all.

You do well, I counseled my soul, to pause here, to take in account the unaccountable power of this newborn image, a face just issuing from a womb of stone, all but lost in time, scored and scalded by weathers.

The small medallion, no larger than a hand's palm, is pressed like a stigma on the imagination of the unborn and the dead, on all who perilously and vulnerably walk the gauntlet of the living.

It has come to this, I thought. A face which once signaled the beginning now would seem to signal the onset of the end, or an hour perilously near the end. Set up long ago on a headland by a few peaceable monks, a guerdon, a legacy signifying peace, all, all is changed. The face has become a very Medusa, a Gorgon, a nuclear Chimera.

The gentle face of new beginnings has become a clock face, warning of mere minutes before midnight, the face of the nuclear countdown.

In America that face of Christ, like a brand on the soul, is impressed in fire on the incumbents of the Christian White House, the Christian Pentagon, the nuclear think tanks and bunkers and bases. In such places Christians, as is said, are "doing their thing." Within walking distance of the living, highly qualified scientists and engineers seriously envision the end of the world. Their ideology and weaponry are hyphenated horrors.

And they pursue their crimes, as many among them assert straight-faced, in honor of the face of Christ. The end of the world, they assure us, is a religious undertaking of the religious West. Let the godless take note.

Christians, I reflected, have honored the face in numberless icons, in worship and prayer and vows. We have also, alas, committed unspeakable crimes while invoking that face, have shielded ourselves from consequences behind that face.

And now Christians would obliterate all faces—in virtue of that face. Thus in cold point of fact, we are coldly informed. The end of the world will be a religious act.

Such folly is so near madness, near the end of all art, the end of all life, as to impel us for sweet sanity's sake, back to our beginnings.

I turned away, toward the ruined sanctuary. I saw then something else, something implied powerfully in the setting. The monks of Caher Island, raising their small chapel, did not place the image of Christ within its walls, under its roof. The standing stone was set at distance from the sanctuary, out of doors, facing the sea, exposed to the wild weathers, unprotected, taking its chances against ice and fire, season and century.

Clinging to their inhospitable island like sea birds to a cliff, lost to the world and its bloody ways, seeking in solitude the Spirit of wisdom and self-knowledge—what a healing the monks offered—and offer! Yin and yang, faith and compassion, gathering into one the fragments of soul, fragments of community. They made peace with the warring halves of our humanity, whose divisions and wounds are our present travail.

Fourteen centuries later, the monks may even have worked such healing for me.

For us? We must resist with all our powers the apocalypticism that would make of gentle Christ the warrior of a mad Christian star war.

33

Transfigured

Caryll Houselander

Christ seems to have fallen in love with our suffering, so passionately has he laid hold of it and made it his. He is known to the whole world as the Man of Sorrows. Yet he came to give us life, life full of joy. It was not with our suffering that Christ fell in love, but with us. He identified himself so wholly with our suffering, because our lives are necessarily made up of it. It is the inescapable consequence of sin. No one can escape it; everyone must somehow either make friends with suffering or be broken by it. No one can come close to another, let alone love him, without coming close to his suffering. Christ did far more, he wed himself to our suffering, he made Death his bride, and in the consummation of his love, he gave her his life. Christ has lived each of our lives, he has faced all our fears, suffered all our griefs, overcome all our temptations, labored in all our labors, loved in all our loves, died all our deaths.

He took our humanity, just as it is, with all its wretchedness and ugliness, and gave it back to us just as his humanity is, transfigured by the beauty of his living, filled full of his joy. He came back from the long journey through death, to give us his Risen Life to be our life, so that no matter what suffering we meet, we can meet it with the whole power of the love that has overcome the world. "I have said this to you, so that in me you may find peace. In the world, you will only find tribulation; but take courage, I have overcome the world" (John 17:33).

He has come back as spring comes back out of the ground, renewing the earth with life, to be a continual renewing of life in our hearts, that we may continually renew one another's life in his love, that we may be his Resurrection in the world. We are the resurrection, going on always, always giving back Christ's life to the world.

🖎

34

Be Kind to Prophets

Malcolm Boyd

The season of Lent portrays the dark night of the soul as a basic element in religious or spiritual experience. Psalm 51 says: "A broken and contrite heart, O God, you will not despise." A basic element is that in Lent we are invited to remember that we are dust, and to dust shall we return. In writing these meditations I invoke the spirit of my book "Are You Running with Me, Jesus?" And as I approach my 90th birthday in June, I invite you to join me in a bit of Lenten meditating.

Prophets are rare creatures. In Lent, we should strive to hear them, be kind and open. Try to understand that beneath their sometime outer hardness and obstinacy is an acute sensitivity and tenderness, a genuine openness to God's spirit.

To a Prophet Dying Young

It wasn't easy knowing you or even hearing you. I felt, in fact, that you were often strong-willed, uncharitable, and impolite.

I saw you pouring out your life. I resented that, too, as I safely clutched my own. Yes, I heard the criticism and on occasion even joined in. When I opposed you it was because what you said and did cut painfully against my mask, security and sense of being. The truth is I miss you very much. You wouldn't want me to wish you "peace" in any conventional way. Frankly, I could never think of you in any misalliance with a false truth or easy compromise.

Yet I do, with all my heart, wish you peace with deep restlessness, a cock crowing at dawn to announce battle and love to heal the necessary wounds.

To a Prophet Dying Old

You had mellowed, they all said, before you died. I question what I know they meant by "mellowed." Softened to the point of atrophy? Sold out for final honors? Quit keeping up with new thoughts and, indeed, thinking them?

I saw and heard you the week before you died. You were as exasperating as ever to everything in me that wanted to be complacent. You rubbed me the wrong way when you bore down, ungraciously I felt and with unneeded force on some highly sensitive areas in my life. You tenaciously caught hold of some issues we just don't talk about.

In other words, you were as independent, strong-willed, unrelenting and saintly as always. You made my blood flow faster, nettled my slumbering conscience, opened up my caved-in thoughts and dragged me outside my wall-to-wall carpeted ghetto. Where did this lead? To involvement with raw sunlight, new ideas and raw commitments.

Damn it, I wanted you to leave me alone. Yes, I resented you and your coming. When you forced me to look honestly at myself and my world, you shook me hard once again. I must admit this was needed. But that didn't mean I liked it. The embers of old fires still burned me when, seeking comfort and release, I came too close.

🖋

35

Fifteen Stations in the Passion According to Mark

Julia Alvarez

As a young Catholic girl, one of my favorite devotions was saying the Stations of the Cross. The exercise appealed to me, a restless church-bound girl, because unlike other forms of prayers—in which we knelt before an image, stationary, gazing on passively—the Stations of the Cross involved actual movement. We walked from station to station, stood and contemplated, knelt and prayed, before moving on. There were fourteen stations in all, fourteen earmarked places in the Passion of Jesus where the suffering spilled over. These particular moments in the Passion were depicted on the walls of most Catholic churches, seven on each side, all the way from the altar down to the front entrance and then back up the other side to the altar. What we were doing, in fact, was accompanying Jesus on his way to Calvary. Almost two thousand years after his death, we were not going to leave him to suffer all by himself again.

But I became especially fascinated with the stations as a young immigrant girl when we moved to a parish in Queens, New York, that had a small, woodsy grove where one could say the Stations of the Cross outdoors.

The church itself was a huge warehouse of a building surrounded by an endless parking lot that stretched all the way to the playground of the Catholic school my sisters and I were attending. To one side of this parking lot, at the margins of the church property, lay the shady grove, which was mostly unused. The grass between the stations was occasionally mowed; the bird droppings hosed off in the summer. In the winter no one remembered to shovel the walk or dust the snow off the stones. Indoors, warm and cozy, hung the elegant, framed stations with nearby pews for comfortable kneeling in prayer. Since the grove was somewhat secluded and heavily shaded, I felt a pang of fear as I climbed the steps through a break in the bedraggled bushes. What if a mugger might be crouching behind *Jesus is helped by Simon* (5th station) or *Jesus is stripped of his garments* (10th station) who would relieve me of my garments and make me undergo suffering—which was really much better endured in the spirit than in the flesh.

Inside the garden a stone path wound round in a circle marked by the fourteen stations, beginning with the first depicting *Jesus being condemned to death*. Then came *Jesus bearing his cross, Jesus falling the first time*, and one of my favorites, the fourth, *Jesus meeting his mother*. Two stations later *Jesus meets Veronica*, another favorite, and this connection with women continued at the eighth station, in which *Jesus speaks to the women*. Through the trees, across the parking lot, inside the church, his back to the congregation (this was 1962, pre–Second Vatican Council's changes), surrounded by male attendants and altar boys, the priest intoned the mass.

But out here in the deserted garden there was female access to the Christ being worshiped indoors. Those tender moments—a mother weeping at the sight of her beaten, broken son; a young woman wiping the blood, sweat, and tears from his suffering face; a group of desolate women reaching toward their bruised and abused teacher who is bearing the cross on which he will shortly be put to death—stirred me. I lingered before these images and reached to dust the snow from Jesus' anguished face much as Veronica had done with her veil.

Despite my racing heart, I loved saying the stations in this dark and gloomy spot, which, I was convinced, was what the Garden of Gethsemane must have been like. Perhaps also, having recently fled the dictatorship of Trujillo in the Dominican Republic, dazed and traumatized by the months of terror that had preceded our exodus, I now had some glancing acquaintance with the visceral fear and loss that brimmed over in those fourteen awful moments. As my young faith began to be tested and my lapsing from the Catholicism of my childhood began, this was one place I felt close to what I've since learned the Passion story is all about.

Forty-five years later, returning to contemplate the Passion as presented in the Gospel of Mark, I'm immediately struck by the absence of women in his account of Christ's suffering on the way to Calvary. But if this is true of the Passion itself, Mark frames his account with two incidents of women ministering or attempting to minister to the physical body of Christ. Before the suffering starts, there is the woman in Bethany who pours her alabaster jar of expensive ointment over Jesus' head despite the protests of some guests who think this is a waste of money. After Christ utters his last cry and dies, the evangelist mentions that "there were women watching from a distance," the very same women who will later go to his tomb to anoint him, only to find him gone. Instead, a young man in a white robe will tell them what those wonderful angels in Bethlehem thirty-three years earlier told the poor shepherds, *Do not be afraid.* But of course, they are terrified, just as I was terrified every time I rounded the grove and spied a lengthening shadow as the sun went behind a cloud, just as my parents had been terrified each time the black Volkswagens of the secret police climbed up our driveway and surrounded our house at night. The spirit is willing but the flesh is weak, hungry, in pain, tired, and terrified. Who wouldn't bolt, betray, break, or emigrate when the horror shows up in their own lives?

That is why Mark, the grimmest of the evangelists, frames the Passion with these two instances of female tenderness—the only consolation we will get from him—as if to contain it. "Mankind cannot bear very much reality," as T. S. Eliot reminds us in the *Four Quartets*. Perhaps that is why in reading Mark's

Passion, I revert to that old favorite framework of the Stations of the Cross: a way to take in the suffering in small "sound bites" because truly we cannot bear this horrible story in its full impact.

And so, I propose to stop at fifteen moments in the Passion of Mark. These are not the traditional stations I knew as a girl, many of which are not moments in Mark anyhow—all the encounters with women I mentioned above, for example. They are instead moments where I feel the brimming over of feeling or insight in reading the text, places where the eye lingers, or the hand absently reaches out to stroke the page. How to bear so much painful reality? Stations, like stories, offer a way to parcel out and mitigate the heart of darkness, string through the labyrinth of suffering that breaks us all, every last one of us, if we are to believe the Passion according to Mark.

Station One

Jesus is anointed by the woman at Bethany. Some begrudge this "waste."

If by the Passion we mean the suffering of Jesus, it begins here in what is seemingly the lull before the storm. Be watchful, he has cautioned in the chapter preceding this account of his dinner in Bethany. Be watchful, lest the lord of the house come suddenly and find you sleeping. The dread in his own heart must be kicking in. Beyond the warm circle of friendship at this table, a plot is afoot; the high priests and scribes are looking for a way to kill him.

But here in Bethany, for this evening, recounted in Mark 14, friends are gathered together, affirming fellowship, a supper prefiguring the last supper. The lamps are lit, the women come in and out to check on what is needed; the smells of cooking waft in from the yard; the soft murmur of conversation. For the moment violence and betrayal seem far away. In one of those expansive gestures of fond devotion, an unidentified woman pours "an alabaster jar of very costly ointment of nard" on Jesus' head. How sweet to feel a soft hand in his hair as he braces himself for the end!

But his friends and supporters begrudge the gesture, even calculating how much money has been wasted: "more than three hundred denarii." Money that might instead be given to the poor, they point out. This is the mantle of righteous goodness that cloaks a stingy soul. Have they factored into their calculations that he is about to sacrifice his only life, worth a lot more? It has to be a needle in the heart to be faced with this smallness of spirit just at the moment when Jesus must yearn for evidence that he is leaving behind strong, big-hearted disciples and followers who can embody the spirit of his life.

It's also a sneaky smallness. For the disciples do not grumble openly about the gesture. They scold the woman. But Jesus defends her, not as one would expect, by taking up the question of his deserving. After all, as their Messiah, isn't he entitled to much more than three hundred denarii worth of perfume? But to respond in this way would be to trade in their currency, to embrace their mentality of nickel-and-diming in order to prove his worth. Instead, he asks simply, "Why do you trouble her? She has performed a good service for me." Her glorious, tender gesture shows more vision than their righteous calculations. This is the anointment he won't be getting at his death. For later, when the women come to his tomb to anoint him, they will not find him there.

In fact, this woman without a name has seen something his trained disciples have missed. She has recognized the Messiah, a title that, after all, means "the anointed one." In Mark, these sideline figures without names or credentials are often the ones who surprise us.

Be watchful, he has told them, but they are already

asleep. They have not been transformed, after all. This is the first of many betrayals to come.

Station Two

The Last Supper. One who dips into the dish with Jesus will betray him.

Here is another supper, this one more staged.

First, two apostles are sent ahead to procure the room by means of instructions that sound a bit like a treasure hunt: "Go into the city, and a man carrying a jar of water will meet you [instead of a woman? water instead of expensive perfume, three hundred denarii's worth?]; follow him, and wherever he enters, say to the owner of the house, 'The Teacher asks, Where is my guest room where I may eat Passover with my disciples?'" These are the kind of instructions the apostles relish—doable deeds, details falling in place, an in-group feel to the whole production. Self-important little men moving and shaking. The arrangements click into place. Just like the boss said.

And so, that night, they sit down at the table, a tight fraternity "in the know," with seeming power to bring about results. Instead, they hear shocking news. Jesus says, "One of you will betray me." They respond not with concern for the victim, Jesus, but for themselves. "Surely, not I?" The response recalls Lady Macbeth's exclamation upon hearing that her guest, King Duncan, has been murdered during the night. "What, in our house?" The king's death is not the tragedy but the fact that it should happen under her roof. "Too cruel anywhere," Banquo reminds her.

When the apostles persist in wanting to know who it is, Jesus responds that his betrayer is "one who is dipping bread into the bowl with me." It is one thing to betray a stranger, or acquaintance, or even a friend. But the poignancy is brought home with this detail. Jesus' betrayer is someone who is intimate with him. They don't just eat; they eat from the very same dish.

My husband, who worked in an eye hospital in the West Bank for a year, tells how occasionally he would be invited out to the countryside by a grateful patient to eat a meal at a tribal household. He was struck by the intimacy of eating together. It was not just a shared meal, each one serving himself on his separate plate.

Everyone was actually eating from the same plate. "You're exchanging body fluids," he explains it. Back in my own past, I met an Amish family who was "shunning" a daughter who had married outside the faith. The young woman could visit the household but never again would she be allowed to eat at its table. In our fast-food nation, we tend to forget that eating together is an intimate act—a sacred, if secular, sacrament.

One who is dipping bread into the bowl with me. The devil is in the details. Betrayal is not just a momentary act but also a betrayal of all the intimacies we have shared. How much more painful is that larger loss. It were better for Judas if he had never been born, even if he is helping bring about a prophecy.

But wait. The one who will betray him, Jesus says, is one who dips into the bowl with him. Aren't they all at the table, presumably eating and dipping into the dish with him? They are right to ask, Surely, not I? The answer is yes. All of them will betray him before the night is out.

What strikes me is what follows this announcement. The one who will betray him is not exposed and cast out. In fact, he, too, is given the bread and wine of that first communion. For Judas, it must be astonishing; he has been found out, but he has not been cast out. This is a new, more expansive love than any one of them could have dreamed up or is yet capable of.

Station Three

Jesus tells his disciples they will all fail him. Peter pro-tests very forcefully.

But Peter is absolutely sure that he will not betray his Lord. Didn't Jesus himself say that Peter is the rock on which the church will be built? He is ready to die for Jesus, he insists with passionate intensity, and hearing him say so, the others fall in.

They mean it. They really do. And they are right to affirm "the better angels of their nature," to quote Abraham Lincoln. What is best in us must be given voice or it ceases to exist. Even in as dark a book as Cormac McCarthy's novel *The Road*, where the world is destroyed and the few survivors are tooth and nail, hunting each other down, the boy who travels with his father toward a destination never named keeps asking his dad, "We're the good guys, right? The keepers of the light." We have to fan those dying embers—if for no other reason than to keep alive in ourselves the memory of that saving grace.

Perhaps it's as simple as that, why Jesus keeps bringing up the fact of his betrayal again and again. It gives the apostles the opportunity to posit their loy-alty, their love for him. To keep the embers of faith alive, embers that might later flare into flames of faith and love. Especially when the apostles remember that Jesus knew that they would fail him, but still he kept them close. He saw the worst devils of their nature and still—as with Judas at the last supper—he did not throw them off.

But his constant mention of betrayal is also one of many reminders in Mark that Jesus is flesh and blood; he is suffering like any man. It is a pebble in his shoe, a bump he needs to keep going over. These intimates who break bread with him and have followed him for years will betray him.

Jesus knows the truth and says so, stripping away feel-good promises, lies we tell others and ourselves. It is part and parcel of his refusal later to take the drug of wine mixed with myrrh that might blunt the agony of being nailed to a cross. He refuses to operate on any other level than the truth about himself and others. We must see things for what they are. We must see into our hearts of darkness even as we affirm that we are children of the light.

Station Four

Jesus calls out, "Abba, Father . . . remove this cup from me."

Jesus is shuddering, shaken, distressed. "I am

deeply grieved, even to death," he confesses to the three apostles he has chosen to accompany him. He throws himself on the ground. This is powerful, visceral, physical fear. Jesus is overcome.

The anticipation of suffering can break a person. The Buddhists call it the second arrow. The first is the pain itself, but the second is the mental anguishing over the pain. My uncle, who was arrested by the secret police and survived six months in the torture prisons in the Dominican Republic, later recalled that the worst torture was the constant dread, not knowing what would happen, but imagining the worst.

And Jesus knows what will happen. He has been talking about it constantly. But now that the hour has almost come, he loses heart. "Abba!" he cries out. "Father!" This is the only place in Mark's Gospel where Jesus addresses God by calling him Father. It is the cry of a terrified child.

This terrified cry is followed so quickly by Jesus' bowing to his fate that it's easy to think, that's right, he is the Son of God. He knows better. But part of being a terrified child is to lose all sense of agency. "Yet, not what I want, but what you want." This utterance is scarier than we think, a total surrender of his own power. Do with me as you will. Is this something we want to hear from a leader?

Of course not. We want him to "rage, rage against the dying of the light," as Dylan Thomas urges his own dying father. Our leaders should be powerful people who put up a fight. They should "not go gentle into that good night." Why would an evangelist show Jesus in such a vulnerable light? Doesn't he want to round up converts, believers? Furthermore, how does Mark even know what Jesus prays when no one is watching, when no one will stay up with him?

Unlike the sleeping disciples, Mark is staying awake, and as we read his words, so are we. This is the good news of the Gospel, an awful one to be sure. Robert Desnos, the surrealist French poet who died in a concentration camp, wrote that the task of being a human being is not only to be one's self, but to become each one. Through an act of the imagination, which some call faith, we become this suffering man.

But what a time to become Jesus—at his worst, most broken moment!

Station Five

Jesus asks his apostles to stay up with him. Three times he wakes them, and three times they fall asleep.

What else can Jesus ask for at this moment of utter terror but the solace of friendship, human warmth and company? "Sit here while I pray."

He then selects three of them, Peter, James, and John, to form yet another ring of protection and company. "Remain here, and keep awake."

In anguish after trying to pray, Jesus goes back to find them all sleeping—including the very same Peter who minutes earlier protested that he would die for his friend. It is no accident that Mark has Jesus single him out with the question, "Simon, are you asleep?"

Simon? Earlier, when Jesus had established the Twelve, he had renamed Simon, Peter. A new name for a new life. But by calling him by his old name, Jesus lets us understand that Simon has not been changed into Peter, after all.

Three times, or actually five, counting the two earlier instances in this same passage, Jesus finds all of his apostles asleep. Be watchful and wakeful, he has been telling them in preparation for this moment. But even as he chides them, he understands that they really mean to be better. "The spirit is eager, but the flesh is weak." Years ago when I was teaching poetry in the schools, a young student in tenth grade, Katie, wrote this poem:

Why is it
I reach for the stars
but I never make it
past the front door?

Katie, girl, I wanted to say, welcome to the human condition. We're all torn among our daily responsibilities, our very real creaturely needs, our limitations, and our far-reaching, star-catching dreams. To give up on that struggle is to become a diminished person, flesh without a chance of ever becoming spirit.

Interestingly, this summons to wake up is a strain in many religions. Rumi, the Sufi poet, urges us, "Do not go back to sleep." Lord Krishna rallies the sleepy Arjuna to arise and join the fray of an awakened life. One of my favorite stories of the Buddha tells how, after he becomes famous, many learned men come to visit him trying to figure out who exactly Buddha is.

"Buddha, are you a god?" they ask him.

"No, I am not a god," the Buddha replies.

"So are you a saint?" they ask.

"No," the Buddha replies, "I am not a saint."

Finally they ask, "So what are you, Buddha?"

And the Buddha says, "I am awake." We are not

gods or saints. The word has to be made flesh. Not just the eager spirit, but also the weary flesh; it takes both to be awake.

The final time Jesus wakes them, it is already too late. The hour has come. His betrayer is near. Had they kept watch, they might have warned him. There might have been a little window in there to get away, to avoid being seized in the middle of the night. In our Latin American dictatorships, late-night squads would haul off the suspect, who would disappear without a trace. A new term entered our vocabulary, to be disappeared. As if he had never been born. The deepest sleep of all, one that Jesus warned would be the legacy of the man who betrays him.

It turns out that while Jesus' followers slept, others have stayed awake, others who come under the cover of darkness wanting to do away with Jesus as if he had never been born. This is an addendum to the Buddha story. It turns out it is not enough to be awake. To what end do we put our wakefulness? In "Ars Poetica," Czeslaw Milosz recognizes that the power of poetry can be used for good and bad purposes:

The purpose of poetry is to remind us
how difficult it is to remain just one person,

for our house is open, there are no keys in the
        doors,
and invisible guests come in and out at will.

What I'm saying here is not, I agree, poetry,
as poems should be written rarely and reluctantly,
under unbearable duress and only with the hope
that good spirits, not evil ones, choose us for their
        instrument.

We must hope and pray that our wakefulness is in
the service of what is good and just. "Lord, make me
an instrument of thy peace," begins that old prayer
attributed to Saint Francis of Assisi. Instruments of
peace in the wrong hands can become weapons of
mass destruction. In our time we have seen a president transform a whole nation into the latter.

Station Six
*Judas betrays Jesus. "Rabbi!" he greets him and kisses
him.*

Here is the man who should never have been born.
Judas betrays Jesus, addressing him as Rabbi, giving him a kiss. This sharpens the edge of betrayal—
achieving it by the very gestures that signal intimacy

and trust, gestures like the earlier one at the table, dipping into the same bowl with Jesus. A coward's way.

Why does Judas betray Jesus? Mark never explains. The high priests promise to give Judas money, but this reward is only mentioned after he has gone to them, and quickly passed over. But that does not seem to have been his motivation. To be able to explain a horrible deed with a motive, however flimsy, reduces the horror. But Mark's silence on the matter is like Iago's silence when Othello asks him why he has "thus ensnared my soul and body?" A silence that is eerie, inhuman.

It would be more bearable to hear an excuse, however flawed. Instead, Judas disappears from the narrative with that kiss. It is odd that he does not follow through on his betrayal by being part of the rigged-up proceedings that are about to take place in the high priest's house. Why is he not one of the witnesses who are brought in to give false testimony? Is he just a pawn of the plot, used to fulfill a prophecy?

Jesus does not respond to the kiss or greeting of "Rabbi!" He matches Judas's silence with his own. So does Mark. As if Judas were not before him, as if indeed he had never been born.

ALL SHALL BE WELL

Station Seven

Jesus' supporter draws a sword and cuts off the ear of the slave of the high priest.

Jesus is seized and bound, but he does not put up a struggle. Instead, one of his supporters starts the violence. Again, have they learned nothing from him?

"Have you come out with swords and clubs to arrest me as though I were a bandit?" Jesus accuses his accusers. In fact, he will be crucified with two robbers, as if he were a common criminal. But he refuses to fight back or to hide or to flee. Now begins the great unveiling of who he is. And the unveiling of his accusers: they are cowards who could have seized him at any time, openly, in broad daylight. Instead, they come for him under the cover of night.

But his supporters are similarly cowardly. Whom do they strike? The slave of the high priest. The old Marxist saw: the boss kicks the worker, the worker goes home and kicks his wife, his wife kicks the child, and the child kicks the dog.

Jesus nips the violence in the bud. There will be no fighting. It is enough. From here on, Jesus surrenders himself to what is coming. He grows quieter and quieter as the Passion proceeds. "Have you no answer?" the high priest asks him in the ensuing interrogation that night. "Have you no answer?" Pilate asks the following day.

Violence is a violation of the effort to communicate. There are no answers in this kind of a world.

Station Eight

A certain young man who had been following him is seized and he flees naked, leaving his linen garment behind.

Even in the grimmest of Shakespeare's tragedies there are moments of comic relief: the drunken porter in Macbeth, the fool in King Lear.

Who is this fellow? Why is he wearing only a linen garment over his bare skin? It is a chilly night. A little later, Peter will be warming himself in front of a fire in the courtyard of the high priest's house.

This fellow has been following Jesus, making a show of his allegiance, like spiritual groupies who showcase their faith, dressed in ashes and sackcloth, lying on a bed of nails. But when the moment comes, the young devotee turns on his heels, terrified, leaving his garment behind!

This moment recalls the stripping away by Jesus of Peter's promises and avowals, a stripping that will continue throughout the Passion until that linen garment reappears as the shroud in which Joseph of Arimathea will wrap the body of Jesus. And that young man will be recalled in the young man sitting inside the tomb wearing a white robe. None of us will get away scot free, after all.

Station Nine

The chief priests and the elders and scribes bring forward false witnesses. The proceedings end with the high priest tearing his clothing, condemning Jesus.

Late night, a rigged-up court, a travesty of a legal proceeding; the false witnesses don't agree, the accused won't talk. The high priest condemns the prisoner as a blasphemer and only as an afterthought asks the rest of the council, "What is your decision?"

In fact, "Why do we still need witnesses?" the high priest asks rhetorically, tearing his robe, a stripping we've seen before. But this stripping is not an effort to bring to light some essence or truth. As with other symbols and gestures—the kiss, the dipping into the bowl—this gesture is a show; it smacks of manipulation, a histrionic ploy. This is what it means to live in a fallen world; the very means by which we communicate in order to understand and clarify are corrupted and destroyed.

Why can't this proceeding wait until morning? For the same reason that those who arrested Jesus did not do so openly when he was in the Temple teaching. But is this legal? Mark underscores that "all the chief priests, the elders, and the scribes were assembled." They all judged that he deserved death. "The chief priests and the whole council." In Mark's Passion there are no dissenting voices, no one of two robbers repenting, no friends at the foot of the cross weeping, no Veronica wiping Christ's face. This is a dark and terrifying world in dire need of salvation.

It does seem amazing that a seventy-one-member council could be assembled at night during festival time without a single absence. Did no one go out of town for the holiday? Of course, this smacks of a set-up, albeit a sloppy one; those false witnesses should have been coached more carefully so their testimony would agree. But Mark follows this death verdict by "all" with the smaller denomination of only "some" who mock him. Later, Joseph of Arimathea, "a respected member of the council, who was also himself waiting expectantly for the kingdom of God," takes courage to go to Pilate to ask for the body of Jesus to bury. Was he one of the "all" assembled at the high priest's house, swept up by the mob mentality we'll see later at Pilate's house, that juggernaut that destroys individual conscience? Did Joseph see the light only after an internal cock crowed and he realized what he had done? I'm sure some in that room were too afraid to object. Then, too, it's important to remember that often those we call evil consider themselves just. They, too, are swept up with the righteousness of their cause. That is why we hope and pray that good spirits, not evil ones, choose us for their instrument.

As for the proceedings themselves, Jesus does not respond to the first accusation that is made, albeit by false, contradictory witnesses. He is accused of saying that he will destroy the Temple made with hands and build another not made with hands, a wacky claim that should have landed him in whatever equivalent there was to a loony bin, not in the Place of the Skull. From early on in his ministry Jesus has made clear to his apostles and followers that he is not interested in temporal, ecclesiastical power—temples made with hands. When the council cannot nail him on that one, the high priest asks him if he is the Christ, the son of the Blessed One. Interestingly enough, the question is not, as with the first accusation, "Do you say that you are the

Christ?" Instead, he is asked, "Are you the Messiah?" And Jesus replies, "I am."

Jesus has unveiled himself before his accusers. Placed beside the figure of the high priest tearing his clothing in a show of rage, we are shown the difference between a temple made with hands and one made without hands.

Station Ten

Peter denies knowing Jesus three times. The cock crows. He remembers Jesus' words and throws himself down and cries.

All the other disciples have deserted Jesus, but Peter follows him into the courtyard of the high priest. He must be given credit for that. He is less a coward than the rest of us.

But he is surrounded. He has no one to help bolster his courage. Or rather, there is someone. Mark juxtaposes Peter's denial to Jesus' open declaration before the entire council. But Peter has reverted back to Simon, still fast asleep in an internal Garden of Gethsemane.

When the cock crows upon his third denial, Peter remembers Jesus' prediction about his betrayal and he throws himself down just as Jesus did in the

Garden of Gethsemane, a mirroring gesture of true despair. Peter has woken up, meeting Jesus on that ground zero, that broken place.

But Peter will get another chance. In a world where there is forgiveness—unlike this chilly, benighted courtyard—there is always one more cock crow, one more chance to turn again, to find courage, to return to the circle of community, to the love that will not give up on us. In this sense the cock's crow is not an announcement of betrayal but a wakeup call. Jesus will not deny Peter. No wonder the serving girl recognizes something in Peter, just as the woman with her alabaster jar in Bethany recognized something about Jesus. These sideline figures, as I mentioned before, have an eye for spirit.

If Judas disappears from Mark's Gospel with a kiss, we last see Peter lying on the ground in tears.

This is the rock on which a whole church will be built.

Station Eleven

Jesus is brought before Pilate with the charge that he claims to be King of the Jews. Pilate is unconvinced, but he gives the crowd the choice, Jesus or Barabbas. They choose.

It has been a busy time for the council of the chief priests, the elders, and the scribes. After their late-night proceedings they meet again, now in the light of day. No mention is made of their earlier gathering, so this morning meeting must be the showcase hearing in which Jesus is openly accused, everything above board. Presumably, the witnesses have had a chance to coordinate their conflicting testimonies of the night before and the high priest's wife has mended his torn robes.

Interestingly, though the late-night court condemned Jesus to death, this "whole council" decides to hand Jesus over to Pilate instead. From Pilate's questioning we learn that the charge has been changed to Jesus' claim that he is "the King of the Jews." A savvy political spin to make the authorities nervous, no doubt. The Romans are, after all, occupiers in this country. Think Iraq, think Americans worried about civil war, uprisings, terrorist bombings. And it's festival time, a time of crowds, a time when riots are likely to break out, a good time to release a prisoner, a safety valve to prevent the buildup of resentment from exploding into full revolt. In fact, the prisoner in question, one Barabbas, was imprisoned along with some insurgents during an uprising. Pilate is in a tricky position; he does not want trouble. The entire council shows up at his door, the movers and shakers who can manipulate public opinion. They've brought in someone who is claiming to be the king of this occupied land.

But, come now! *This* is the King of the Jews? By his constant repetition of the phrase, one senses that Pilate is mocking not Christ, but his accusers. This beaten, silent man is hardly insurgent material. Barabbas is by far the more dangerous of the two to the state. King of the Jews? When questioned, Jesus doesn't even try to defend himself. "You say so," he answers the charge. No wonder Pilate is amazed. He knows this poor wreck of a man is innocent. "What evil has he done?" he asks the members of the crowd, as if they are the ones under interrogation. But there is no reasoning with them. The chief priests have stirred them up.

Pilate is trapped. He has offered the crowd a choice. He is an occupier wanting to satisfy the crowd. And so he ends up crucifying an innocent man while remaining technically clear of having condemned him. But later that day, when Joseph of Arimathea comes to ask permission to bury the body, Pilate is again amazed that this King of the Jews would already be dead. He summons the centurion for confirmation. These are the head scratchings of a man in an occupied land, all right. A man unsettled by the day's events. A man unsure of what he has done. *King of the Jews*, he muses over the phrase. "It was they who said so," Pilate can tell himself, passing the buck on to the crowd and the entire council. But Jesus' words were clear, "You say so." The buck stops here, as Peter discovers—on the ground, weeping bitter tears.

Station Twelve

The whole cohort clothes Jesus in purple, crowns him with a wreath of thorns, beats him, mocks him as King of the Jews, then leads him out to be crucified.

What pleasure is there in humiliating a man who already has a death sentence on his head?

These are soldiers, supposedly disciplined creatures, not the madding crowd outside. Again Mark emphasizes that "the whole cohort" joined in the fun.

"Hail, King of the Jews!" The cruel joke continues. A mock crowning, soldiers going down on their knees.

We look at images from Abu Ghraib and our hearts stop. The torturers are young men and women—they look like students in my classrooms, like local kids we've watched grow up, like our own sons and daughters.

They are stacking up naked men in a human pyramid, climbing on them, giving the camera a thumbs up, grinning. Why on earth would they want to record this disgusting moment?

A young woman is hauling a naked man on a leash, his hands tied behind his back. A young man is taunting a kneeling man with an attack dog. A prisoner, a black hood over his head, stands on a box, his genitals wired for electric shocks. This is not interrogation justified by an urgent need to save innocent lives. This is glee at participating in the breaking and the suffering of another human being.

In his book *Unspeakable Acts, Ordinary People: The Dynamics of Torture* John Conroy writes that torturers are ordinary people, most of them decent folks obeying authority. *King of the Jews!* The taunt echoes down from the chambers of the powerful council members to the servants in the courtyard. From Pilate, the governor, to the soldiers who lead Jesus inside the official residence and call up the whole cohort. *King of the Jews!* They echo. Evil is infectious, Conroy concludes. Torturers are ordinary people, many of them relying on the moral leadership of higher ups.

And Mark wants us to see this. He slows down the action. Sentence after breathless sentence is a lash stroke, as if by reading the account, we are both participating in and enduring the humiliation: "And they began saluting him. . . . And they struck his head with a reed. . . . After mocking him . . . they led him out to crucify him."

Mark does not turn away. "I am a human being," Terence, the Roman slave and playwright, wrote. "Nothing human is alien to me." In the Passion according to Mark, we are being forced to acknowledge the horrors inside our own military, our own country, our own religion, our own heart. It's as if those sentences were breaking us down as well, as if we, too, have to end up with Peter, weeping on the ground over our own inhumanity to one another.

Station Thirteen

Jesus is led away to Golgotha to be crucified. . . . Simon of Cyrene is impressed to carry the cross. . . . And Jesus is offered wine mixed with myrrh. . . . And his clothes are divided. . . . Then he is crucified.

The lash strokes continue, most sentences beginning with the conjunction *and*, just when we thought we could bear no more.

Certainly Jesus is faltering under the weight of so much abuse. He can't carry his own cross anymore. A certain Simon of Cyrene is *impressed* to carry it, enlisted by force, a draft of sorts. Simon is coming in from the country; perhaps he has been out working in the fields, not part of the festival crowd. He is an outsider to the action so far, someone presumably known to Mark's readers as the father of Alexander and Rufus—just as later, one of the women who is watching the crucifixion from a distance is identified as Mary, the mother of James the Lesser and Joses.

Why does Mark give us this bit of genealogy at this point in the narrative? He knows the deeds he is describing are cruel and horrible. We, his readers, are beginning to falter under the weight of so much violence. Perhaps this account is too exaggerated? So, Mark offers us living proof, a witness, a way to connect us to the story at a point where we want to back away. Any doubts? Go ask Alexander and Rufus what their father saw.

Was Simon's life utterly changed by this encounter? Did he pass on this story to his two sons, who seem to have become part of the community of readers Mark is addressing in his Gospel? Simon is from

Cyrene, a city in North Africa. Much has been made of this, Simon being considered an African, the first black saint, although at the time of Christ, Cyrene was a Roman city and former Greek colony, not an African nation. Whatever his exact provenance and race, one thing is clear: Simon is not a native of Jerusalem. The outsiders are being let in. The veil of a temple that separates the holy of holies from the hoi polloi is definitely being rent.

Jesus is crucified between two robbers, his offense inscribed on the cross: *King of the Jews.* Now those who mock him bring up all the charges we've heard before, including the original one of Jesus saying that he would tear down the Temple in three days as well as his claim that he is King of Israel. Of course, the chief priests have followed the procession up to Golgotha, the Place of the Skull. They taunt Jesus to come down from the cross, and then they will believe him. This is bogus faith that works by signs, makes conditions, needs proof: the casting of demons, the speaking in tongues, the handling of serpents, the drinking of poison—reason enough to reject the spurious ending in which these claims are made for believers, tacked on to "complete" the Gospel of Mark.

Station Fourteen

Darkness descends on the earth. Jesus calls out, "My God, My God, why have you forsaken me?" Jesus utters a last great cry and dies. The veil in the Temple is split in two. A centurion posted across from the crucified Jesus says, "Truly this man was God's Son!"

Jesus is agonizing on the cross. From the sixth hour (noon) to the ninth hour (three in the afternoon), "darkness came over the whole land." The language is reminiscent of Genesis 1. The Temple veil is being torn asunder just as a newborn tears open his mother's birth canal. Here in the Place of the Skull, that ground zero where all is lost, a new world order is about to be born.

Before he dies, Jesus cries out, "Eloi, Eloi, lema sabachthani? My God, my God, why have you forsaken me?" This is the most terrifying moment in Mark's Passion, worse than the anguish in the Garden of Gethsemane, the late-night arrest, the bogus hearing, the beatings, and the torture. Throughout all those ordeals Jesus' faith remained intact. "Yet not what I want, but what you want," he says, submitting to his Father's will.

But here, Jesus' last intelligible words are a seeming admission that God has abandoned him. It is as if Jesus loses faith. The chief priests and scribes are right: where is God when Jesus needs him? No wonder the later evangelists, Luke and John, report different last words, either intentionally changing Mark's Passion, fearing that the faithful could not bear this much painful reality, or perhaps choosing another among a variety of reports, once more in keeping with the Jesus they want to believe in and promote.

My first encounter with the Passion of Mark was in catechism class. In eighth grade, during Holy Week, Sister Mary Joseph had us read the four evangelists' accounts of the Passion. Saint Mark's version upset me. My hand shot up. *My God, My God, why have you forsaken me?* "Did Jesus stop believing in God?"

"Of course not!" Sister Mary Joseph replied, annoyance straying into her voice. She had me pegged as someone who asked too many questions. Besides, she was racing us toward the resurrection.

Maybe it was my imperfect English? I looked up forsaken in the dictionary. "Abandoned," "deserted." The next class my hand went up again. "Why does Jesus think God has abandoned him?"

"It is not God who has abandoned him, it is humanity."

Sister Mary Joseph was right. It was human-kind—the chief priests, the crowds, and the Roman soldiers—doing these cruel things to Jesus. But then why didn't Jesus say, "My people, my people, why have you forsaken me?"

I don't remember pursuing this line of questioning with Sister Mary Joseph. I must have caught on that it would not yield happy results. But now, forty-five years later, I'm still puzzled and disturbed by Jesus' last words. And I think Mark wants me to be.

Jesus' last words are terrifying. He is calling out in despair. God has forsaken him, the only way that God can forsake us, through his creation, the cruelty and betrayal of our human family. We ache for other words. But all we will hear from Jesus before he dies is one last great cry, an animal noise of suffering, not phrased and contained in language. The veil is rent in the Temple. We've seen this stripping throughout the Passion of Mark, a breaking down of the old paradigms, the temple made with human hands.

This is a dark and terrifying place to have Jesus' life end.

Or so it would seem. But not for those who stay with the mystery, who see with the eyes of the woman at Bethany or the centurion posted in front of the cross. "Truly," this centurion says, "this man was God's Son!"

What truth has this man has seen? The others at the foot of the cross are trying their experiments with a sponge soaked in vinegar, wondering if Elijah will come. Credulous and clueless, they are still waiting for their miracle to happen. But Mark has posted the centurion here, as if to say to us who see only defeat and hear only despair in this Place of the Skull, look again. There is another way to understand this story.

"My God, my God, why have you forsaken me?"

These are the very words that open Psalm 22, the psalm of the righteous sufferer, calling out to God, "My God, my God, why have you forsaken me? . . . Trouble is near and there is no one to help." In one of my copies of the bible, a commercial edition with a back cover that advises "Where to look in the Bible: WHEN you can't go to sleep, WHEN tempted to do wrong, WHEN business is poor, WHEN you are bored." Psalm 22 is recommended WHEN the whole world seems to be against you. It is a summoning, an incantation that ends with a triumphant vision of God's kingdom on earth:

All the ends of the earth shall remember
and turn to the Lord;
and all the families of the nations
shall worship before him.

By reciting the opening words of the psalm at this moment of extreme suffering, Jesus is affirming his faith. In what Mark describes as a "loud cry," which must be hard for a dying man, Jesus proclaims the truth he foretold to the high priests the night before. God and his kingdom will triumph.

But if Jesus is affirming his faith, why doesn't Mark have him finish reciting the psalm, or at the very least, jump to the triumphant ending? Why not eliminate all doubt so we don't have to wonder if this is a proclamation of triumph or an acknowledgment of defeat?

Mark is testing us. Just when we thought that all was lost, the centurion's incredible utterance sends us back to gaze upon this man on the cross. To reconsider Jesus' words. They *are* unfinished. If we want the joyful ending that Psalm 22 promises, it is we who must complete the story.

Beyond this first convert, this amazed centurion, the circle begins to widen. Watching from a distance are the women who have followed Jesus and served him in Galilee, many others who have come up with him to Jerusalem, as well as Joseph of Arimathea, who is also looking for the kingdom of God. A growing congregation, who must take courage and claim the body of the crucified Christ and pass on an amazing story that he is alive.

Station Fifteen
Mary, the Magdalene, and Mary, the mother of James, and Salome go to Jesus' tomb.

The women "brought spices, so that they might go and anoint him." They worried about how to push aside the tombstone. "They saw that the stone . . . had already been rolled back. As they entered the tomb, they saw a young man, dressed in a white robe, sitting on the right side; and they were alarmed. But he said to them, 'Do not be afraid; you are looking for Jesus of Nazareth, who was crucified. He has been raised.'" The women are to tell his disciples, and Peter, that Jesus will meet them in Galilee, as he had promised. But the women "fled from the tomb, for terror and amazement had seized them; and they said nothing to anyone, for they were afraid."

When I was growing up there were only fourteen

stations. The fourteenth and final stop was *Jesus is laid in the tomb*. A gloomy ending, very much in the spirit of the Passion according to Mark, who ends his Gospel with three terrified women fleeing from an empty tomb. "And they said nothing to anyone, for they were afraid." How can this be a way to conclude a story that purports to be good news?

The Catholic Church obviously thought it was not a very good close to the stations. The very year that I discovered the hidden grove, the Second Vatican Council added a fifteenth station: *Jesus rises victorious over death*. It was felt that the crucifixion was pointless without the resurrection. Emphasis should be on the risen Christ. The faithful needed a happier ending.

A similar impulse in the second century after Christ resulted in two alternate endings being tacked on to the Gospel of Mark. Both endings read very much like the conclusion of Psalm 22, with the promise of God's reign on earth. The longer ending concludes with these words: "And they went out and proclaimed the good news everywhere, while the Lord worked with them and confirmed their message by the signs that accompanied it." The shorter alternate ending is also a heartening affirmation: "Jesus himself sent forth through them, from east to west, the holy and imperishable proclamation of everlasting salvation." As for the question of authenticity, the Catholic Church has declared that these additions are canonically authentic, even though they are not authentic in a literary sense.

But as a writer, I want my authenticity to also be literary. Besides, it seems to me that those who tack on these alternate, upbeat endings are missing Mark's point. Ironically, they are acting in the spirit of the fearful women, afraid to pass on the true message they have heard.

Why are these women so afraid? Why shouldn't they be? Even Jesus' right-hand man, Peter, has denied him. These women have been hovering in the sidelines, powerless, seeing what can happen to those who defy authority. We must not be hard on them, as Jesus reminded his followers concerning the woman at Bethany. They are trying to do a good thing. As they walk to the tomb, they are worrying about how they will move the large stone at the entrance. When they get there, the stone is already rolled back. At this point, they might have run off, afraid. But no, they investigate further.

Inside, they find a young man who is described in words that echo Jesus' words about his resurrection to the council of chief priests on the night before he died: "You will see the Son of Man seated at the right of the Power and 'coming with the clouds of heaven.'"

Here we see a young man in a white robe sitting on the right side of Jesus' tomb. He tells them not to be amazed. He gives them the good news. Jesus has been raised. He asks them to pass on this news to the disciples and to Peter, who is now reinstated with his God-given name. The women flee. They say nothing to anyone, for they are afraid. End of story.

But how can it be the end of the story? After all, we know the story. The women must have eventually spoken out. Either that or the risen Jesus met the disciples in Galilee, as he had promised, and there told them the story of the three terrified women. We cannot know what happened, just as we cannot know what it was the centurion saw, but we do know that we have received this story, just as the women received the message from the young man.

Who is this young man in a white robe? Is he an angel? Is he the young follower who fled leaving his garment behind in the hands of one of the council's soldiers? But an even greater amazement than the messenger is his incredible message: Jesus has been raised. This mystery with which Mark ends his Passion leaves us, his readers, struggling to understand, waiting and watching like these women for that moment of faith to seize us so we can pass on this story.

But a story can only go so far. It is not finished until it takes hold in a reader's imagination. A living understanding. The word made flesh. This is a good place to begin—as John does—or to end the good news. Mark's Passion is inconclusive. Like all true stories it washes up on the shores of our understanding, asking nothing less than for us to complete it by changing our lives.

🖎

36

Way of the Cross

Virgil Elizondo

One of the most traditional and popular devotions in the Christian world is the Stations of the Cross. Ancient tradition tells us that after Jesus' Ascension Mary was the first to retrace the steps of her son's passion and death. The church has never required dogmatic assent to this belief; but every generation of Christians, driven by some instinct of faith, has tried to retrace the steps of Jesus to Calvary, discovering that he continues to journey with us in our own passion and way of the cross. In him our own Calvary takes on new meaning.

I have retraced the way of the cross since childhood. In my [former] parish church in Texas, San Fernando Cathedral, it continues to be the most popular devotion. And each year in my present city, San Antonio, merchants stop doing business at noon on Good Friday so that everyone may follow the way of the cross. The world joins with the Holy Father when he takes up the cross in the evening of Good Friday and leads us all in this traditional devotion.

As I make the way of the cross each year, I note that the suffering has not been erased, loneliness continues, and the betrayal and abandonment of friends breaks my heart. The lashes of the whip still go on, the crown of thorns continues to make me bleed, the unjust condemnations make me wonder about divine justice, and the death of innocent victims causes me to cry out: "Lord, why have you forsaken us?" Nothing has changed and there does not seem to be much point in continuing to meditate on the Way of the Cross.

It may indeed seem that nothing changes, indeed that the world is getting worse. But what is changing is my heart. Each time we make the Stations of the Cross we discover more of the drama in the great battle to end all battles: the clash between God's limitless love and our own love—conditioned, limited, and even perverted by material riches and the social demands of this world. But what slow learners we are!

Through the centuries we Christians have preferred to destroy with wars and conquests rather than to build new societies of harmony, mutual help, honest work, reconciliation, and love. War has been far more attractive than peace, and the conquerors have appeared far more attractive than the confessors, prophets, and martyrs.

The history of the Christian world, sad to say, has been a history of every possible kind of warfare. In this century we have witnessed two world wars with Christians killing Christians. The atomic bomb came from a Christian country. Christian countries initiate the massive arms sales to peoples and nations in need of food and medicine. And Christian countries produce the most powerful armies in the world. It seems that the greatness of a human being is measured by his ability to kill other human beings, and our heroes are the military leaders who kill in cold blood anyone who seems to be an enemy.

We are scandalized by the human sacrifices of our Aztec ancestors, but we sacrifice many more people on the altars of modern technological warfare without batting an eye. How many innocent people have died in the wars of Central America or on the streets of Brazil? How many innocent people were killed or buried alive in the war against Iraq? And where are we Christians? What do we have to say about all this?

We continue to glorify the destructive forces of this world. We say our cultures are in good order and committed to equality, justice, brotherhood, science, technology, progress, and human development; but the masses continue to suffer exploitation and die of hunger. We call ourselves civilized and our victims uncivilized. We worry about the disappearance of the Amazon rain forest but we do not worry about the disappearance of its human inhabitants. We debate ecological issues, but we close our eyes to the millions of poor people who live, work, and die in lands contaminated by our radioactive waste.

In the way of the cross the most incomprehensible injustices experienced in my lifetime take on liberative and redemptive significance. Far from justifying the injustices of our world, the way of the cross from Jesus' day to our day continues to rip away the sacred curtain around what is deemed good, attractive, just, and even holy in this world. It shows those things for what they really are: ugly, rotten, even Satanic. At the same time it reveals the ones who are truly God's good and holy ones: those who freely love to the point of giving their lives for others, even for people who betray, abandon, and condemn them to death. They are unjustly condemned to death by those who feel threatened by God's limitless love. The way of the cross continues to reveal the persistent malice of a world dominated by sin and the inexhaustible love of a God who seeks to save us in spite of ourselves.

The Americas have been a font of hope and new life for many people around the world in the last five hundred years. We hope and pray that the God of life will resurrect those other people for whom the Americas have largely been a cross and Calvary. We pray that God may destroy in us everything that leads to the suffering and death of others, turning us into agents of new life rather than of death.

37

Following in Footsteps

Greg Boyle, SJ

"Do you understand what I've just done to you?," Jesus asks, after washing his disciples' feet. From that day forward, the Church has washed the feet of 12 men on Holy Thursday. That is, of course, until Pope Francis celebrated Holy Thursday, not in a Basilica, but in a jail . . . washing the feet of prisoners . . . men, women, and Muslims.

St. Francis of Assisi admonishes us with this: "Don't imitate Jesus. Follow in his footsteps." Jesus doesn't want a fan club ("I have all your records. I go to every concert.") You won't find a single "worship me" in the Gospel. But you'll find a ton of "Follow me."

"Do you understand what I've just done to you?"

We either simply imitate the action—(12 males feet), or we domesticate the message: "Serve others." Don't get me wrong. I like BOTH service AND clean feet. But what Jesus does is more than service and deeper than mimicry.

In washing all the dirt-covered "dedos" of his friends, Jesus achieves this remarkable and intimate connection with his followers. With a humility that erases the daylight separating them, Jesus draws them into a tenderness—"loving them to the end"—so that they can follow in his footsteps. "Only connect," E.M. Forster writes and this can only happen in humility.

"If you're humble, you'll never stumble," Robert, a homie who works at Homeboy Industries, often says . . . and I've adopted it as my own calming mantra. Humility keeps you more interested in being interested than in being interesting. It keeps "Hubris," humility's opposite, at a safe distance. Humility says, "I need healing." Hubris says, "I am the healer."

Miguel walked into my office after a year working at Homeboy Industries. He had graduated from our school and was now taking courses at a local community college at night. At 19 years old, he was a tattooed gang member who began work with us right after release from a detention facility. He had something on his mind. "I discovered something today," he begins. "I discovered that . . . you're my father. Yeah . . . it's nice to have a father."

I was startled by this. "Wow," I told him, "You made my whole damn day right there. I would have thought I had won the lottery if God had handed me a son like you." But it begged the question. "And YOUR father?"

Miguel waves his hand as a dismissal. "Aw . . . he was never there for me. Haven't seen him in like ten years."

Then you can tell when a homie reaches for a snapshot from the family album he'd rather keep closed. "He broke my arm once." He proceeds then to tell me that his father came home from work one day and rushes past Miguel and his kid brother playing in the living room, and enters his bedroom, closing the door. The father emerges minutes later in a rage. "Who stole my batteries?" Well, little Miguel had a toy requiring two batteries. He rummaged through his Dad's drawers and found them. "I did," Miguel squeaks timidly, raising his hand.

Now Miguel begins to quietly sob and it takes a moment for him to finish the story. Miguel's father walked straight up to him, grabbed his arm . . . and snapped it in two. Miguel cries all the more in the telling. Then he says to me, "I was six years old . . . Yeah . . . It's nice . . . finally . . . to have a father." And the daylight separating us—"Service provider . . . service recipient" is erased . . . leaving only a connection born of an awe at what the poor have to carry. The humble connection has its roots not in "reaching" people, but in "receiving" them. And in the receiving, we all get returned to ourselves. Only then can we follow in the footsteps of Jesus.

I flew to Washington, DC to speak to a Congressional Sub-Committee on gangs. I brought Louis and Joe with me. They were older "*vatos*" who did a variety of things at Homeboy. After our testimony, we went to the Holocaust Museum. I encouraged Joe and Louis to walk around the place alone and at their own pace . . . wanting to maximize the experience for them. We met in the foyer at our agreed upon time and the two of them were deeply moved. While debriefing in the lobby, we noticed a desk set up off to the side. A man in his 80's sitting behind it, reading a book. There is an empty chair in front, as if to invite you to sit in it. There is a sign on the desk: "Holocaust Survivor."

"Wow," Joe says, "What would we say to someone

who has suffered so much?" Louis, because he is fearless, dives in, "Well, I'm gonna go talk to him." We tell him to meet us in the gift shop later.

Louis tells us later that the man's name is Jacob. He was 13 when he went to Auschwitz. Both parents killed there. Two sisters executed in front of his eyes. A niece and nephew also murdered. Louis listens. When Jacob is finished, Louis pulls out his business card and hands it to him. "I work at Homeboy Industries. It's the largest gang intervention, rehab and re-entry program in the world. I hope . . . that if you're ever in LA, you'll come visit us."

Jacob studies the card. "I'm 35 years old . . . and half my life, I've been locked up." Jacob scoffs a bit. "American prisons," rolling his eyes, " You have your own room. You sleep on a mattress. You have a pillow. We slept on wooden planks. If you spoke in line, they'd pull you out, and beat you nearly to death."

Louis listens intently, then tells him, "Yeah . . . I was beaten by a gang 'a times in County Jail. Once . . . they beat me so bad . . . I looked like the Elephant Man. Then they threw me naked into a cell and I slept on a metal sheet."

It was at this moment that I intervened. "Let me

see if I got this right, Louis. You were comparing your experience . . . to a Holocaust survivor?" His response was sure and clear-eyed. "No. I wasn't comparing. There is no comparison between his experience and what I've been through." And now, his eyes moisten but his resolve doesn't waver. "No. I wasn't . . . competing . . . with him." A tear runs down his cheek. "I was . . . connecting with him."

"Do you understand what I have just done to you?" Only connect. A discipleship, intimate and humble, which seeks not to "reach people" but to "receive them." No daylight . . . only the following in footsteps.

꒰

38

Foot-Washing of a Different Sort

Sheila Cassidy

I spent Easter at L'Arche, a community of handicapped people and their helpers, which lies in the French village of Trosly Breuil on the edge of the forest outside Compiegne. The community, which began in 1964 with two handicapped men and a gentle French Canadian named Jean Vanier, is now home to two hundred men and women, handicapped and helpers, who live together in *foyers*, ordinary houses, in groups of anything from ten to twenty. As an outsider with little French I often find it difficult to distinguish between the carers and handicapped, for the boundaries are frequently blurred. Perhaps the most important thing that L'Arche has taught me is that labels are of little consequence, for we are all wounded, handicapped in some way or another. Having long feared to come to L'Arche because I thought I could not cope with the mentally handicapped, I find myself absurdly at home, recognizing for the first time that I too am handicapped, hurt and maimed from birth and by circumstance and that this is an acceptable way of being a person.

On Holy Thursday we celebrated the liturgy of the institution of the Eucharist and washing of the feet. I have a deep love of these Holy Week services and for many years have spent the Easter Triduum at Ampleforth, a Benedictine monastery in the North of England where the monks open their doors to share their prayers with a large number of laypeople like me. On Holy Thursday night the abbot and a number of other priests celebrate Mass and as a part of the liturgy they wash the feet of twelve men from the congregation. This washing is a rather stylized affair, with the abbot, girded in a towel, pouring water from a silver jug on a clean pint foot held over a large silver bowl. It is a symbolic act, a ritualized re-enactment of an old story: that Jesus, the night before he was betrayed, rose from the supper table, tied a towel around his waist and washed the feet of his disciples. When he had finished he returned to the table and asked his disciples, "Do you understand what I have done to you?" One can imagine them looking blankly at him and them at each other. What on earth was he doing, he, their rabbi and master, humbling himself to touch their dirty feet, caked in the dust of the Palestine roads? How did he speak to them, I wonder? Gently, or with an undertone of urgency and mild exasperation? This was his last time with them, his last chance to instill in them the principles of a way of living so different from the norm that they still could not grasp it. "Look," he said, "you call me Master and Lord, and rightly, for that's what I am. So if I, your Lord and Master, have washed your feet, so you should wash one another's feet. Do you see? I have given you an example so that you can copy what I have done to you."

That night in L'Arche, in the *foyer* they call Le Val Fleury, I witnessed a re-enactment of this scene that left me spellbound and gave me new insights into Jesus' last, most urgent commandment—that we must love one another just as he had loved us. The evening went on like this: at first we all gathered for Mass, a glorious motley of several hundred people, men, women, and children, the handicapped and the outwardly whole, in a large meeting room. There were readings, hymns and a flute solo, woven into the celebration of the Eucharist, the memorial of Jesus' last supper with his friends. As always at L'Arche the service was long but everyone seemed happy, even toddlers who roamed freely around the church as whim and courage took them. Then came the supper in our *foyer* with forty to fifty people gathered around a long table. There were Luisa from Italy, two Marias from Austria, and a professor of geophysics from Paris who had been born in Vietnam. There was Jean, who began it all, gentle, shabby and full of laughter, and Barbara, his assistant, tiny with shining eyes and mind and wit razor sharp, flitting from language to language as she spoke to the people around her. My neighbor Ted from Toronto, a Jesuit student studying theology in Paris, drawn, like myself, by the magic of this unwieldy family.

After the meal Jean spoke a little of the meaning of our celebration: of Abraham, the first Jew, who had taken his family into an unknown land, a prototype of all who find themselves answering a call into the unknown; and of Moses who led the people of Israel from the slavery of Egypt into the Promised Land. God loved the people of Israel so much that he rescued them and they, in their turn, were to remember their liberation by celebrating the Passover meal; by remembering the story and telling it to their children. And now we were remembering another Passover meal—the last one that Jesus shared with his disciples before he gave himself up for them. Greater love hath no person, man or woman, than to give themselves for the love of another. This is the magic and mystery of our humanity that one man will sacrifice himself for another, in the gift of a life spent in service or in one incredible gesture of love, like that of Maximilian Kolbe, the Polish priest who took the place of a condemned man in the death chambers of Auschwitz. Individually and together we recalled the gifts of the past year. It was hard for me to understand the muttered words of the native French speakers, but now and again I caught the more stilted phrases of foreigners like myself, for whom the gift of love in L'Arche had brought a new dimension to their lives. The halting words of the carers, trying to express what God had meant to them this year, were balanced by the simplicity of the handicapped for whom a gift or trip had been a precious sign that they were loved.

When all had had their turn to speak we moved to another room and arranged ourselves in a great circle for the washing of the feet. A carer and a handicapped man sat in the center of the group, waiting with towel and basin for the ceremony to begin. Then it was the turn of Xavier, the professor from Paris, to speak. Had we noticed, he asked, that St. John had omitted the passage of the Eucharist from his account of the Last Supper? The other gospels related how Jesus had taken bread and broken it and given it to his disciples, telling them that this was his body, given for them. But not John. Instead he told how Jesus had taken a bowl of water and a towel and washed his disciples' feet. He had replaced one story with another. Why? Because they conveyed the same message: that life was about sacrifice, about service, and the love of God must be paid out in love of neighbor. Greater love hath no man than he who pours out his life for another. And life is not just blood given once and for all, it is time and energy, tears and laughter, poured out hourly, daily, over a lifetime.

Impatiently, Michael waited, poised to wash the feet of Patrick, the man seated in front of him. I'm not sure how much he understood of what the professor said. His eyes were fixed on the water and he held the towel in readiness. At last he was allowed to begin. No silver jug and basin here, and certainly no symbolic or ritual ablution! This was the real thing: a washing up bowl, full of warm soapy water with Patrick's foot plunged firmly in. Lovingly, Michael soaped it, up and down, round the heel and then gently between each toe. At last, he was satisfied, and lifted it out onto his lap to dry. Gently he patted the clean skin and separated the toes, drying each one individually. Then the other foot was soaped, rinsed and dried with equal care. I sat fascinated. Here was the carer being tended by his charge. Here was Michael, the simpleton, showing us how to love. It was not just the gentleness, but the rapt concentration and attention to detail. He was showing us in his own way that people are precious, that the human body is wondrously beautiful, to be honored and handled with care. I was reminded of times I had seen nurses at the hospice, washing an unconscious patient with such infinite tenderness that it breaks my heart. This manner of handling the body is for some an instinctive thing, an expression of a love that possesses the carer, driving out natural squeamishness or distaste and replacing it with an innate sense of the holiness of people, of their infinite worth.

I find in this unselfconscious love a very special revelation of God. It struck me the first time I visited

L'Arche and sat up in the gallery at Mass watching the helpers with their charges. The natural tenderness with which they handled the profoundly handicapped touched me deeply. There was something so moving in the contact between the youth and beauty of these carers and the deformed bodies and damaged intellects of their charges. They sat together on a rug at the foot of the altar, arms entwined, stroking the hair and whispering gently in the ear of the person they were holding. I thought of the majority of the profoundly handicapped, hidden in the wards of long-stay hospitals and of the way they are shunned by those of us who are strong and whole. Their very existence poses questions about God and life and human values that we find difficult to answer. And here were these young helpers, so beautiful and full of promise spending their love and vitality upon these broken creatures, with their necks awry, their eyes rolling and their tongues monstrously protruding from their open mouths. As I watched, I remembered anew this fragment of Sidney Carter's poem, which speaks so powerfully of my own work:

> Over this dead loss to society
> you pour your precious ointment.

You wash the feet
that will not walk tomorrow.
Call the bluff and laugh
at the fat and clock-faced gravity
of our economy.

I have a deep sense of the wholeness of the liturgy
at L'Arche—a liturgy in which everyone has their
place. The presence of the handicapped at the foot
of the altar is somehow so right and fitting. They are
there at the heart of the liturgy, given pride of place
at the table. It is difficult to write without sounding
sentimental—perhaps I am—but I find myself so
much more at home here, with this motley of people
and little children wandering about, than I do at my
own parish church. There is a deep sense of reverence
in the congregation that has nothing to do with arriving on time or kneeling up straight in a pew. Mothers
with tiny babies wander in and out, clumsy handicapped men lurch unselfconsciously to their feet and
go out for a while and then return, physically disturb-
ing their neighbors, yet somehow not breaking the
silence. Many of the less severely handicapped act as
acolytes and they too merge into the liturgy. There is
a sense of acceptance of all that makes each person

comfortable and therefore not disturbed by behavior which would be unbearably intrusive in another environment. Truly, that is for me, as Eliot would say, a place where worship is valid.

> You are not here to verify,
> Instruct yourself, or inform curiosity
> Or carry report. You are here to kneel
> Where prayer has been valid. And prayer is more
> Than an order of words, the conscious occupation
> Of the praying mind, or the sound of the voice
> praying.
>
> —T.S. ELIOT, *Little Gidding*

Our foot-washing liturgy took over an hour, but rarely have I been so prayerful and at home among strangers. Each person washed the feet of his or her neighbor; when the water got a bit grey and the towel sodden, a fresh bowl and a dry towel were brought. It was a joy to watch the handicapped for they brought simplicity and seriousness to an act which otherwise might have been banal. From time to time there was laughter which flowed as naturally in the silence as the babies gurgling in church. It was a good time to watch, to pray and to reflect. At one stage in the proceedings I had a strange sense of the beauty of these people. It was not that they were pretty or that they glowed or were illuminated, I just saw them as beautiful—not different. They just looked beautiful to me, their faces full of concentration, gentleness and laughter. I felt as though I were seeing them through God's eyes, and knew briefly how it was that God loves them—each one so different and so precious.

I am conscious that I write rather emotionally about a group of ordinary people who live, love and hate just as the rest of us do. I believe, however, that sometimes one is given a glimpse of a deeper truth about life and people—an eternal truth which lies beyond the immediate. It is not so much that the handicapped and their helpers are special and holy but that their way of life makes the uniqueness and holiness which is innate in humans easier for me to see. I know well that the hospice where I work provides the same experience of revelation for many people. Most of the time I am so close to it that I am blind to the power of what we are doing: a foot-washing of a different sort.

I remember well the night I was given the Sidney Carter poem that I quoted earlier:

All Shall Be Well

> No revolution will come in time
> to alter this man's life
> except the one surprise
> of being loved.

I had been asked to speak to a group of volunteers from the Home Care service in a nearby town. I was so exhausted by pressures of work and a heavy schedule of lectures that I could not face the hour's drive and asked my secretary to take me. We had been invited to supper by the woman involved with the volunteers, and as we sat at the table her husband asked me if I had been "healed" of my experience in prison. Finding the question bewildering and intrusive, I muttered something a bit sharp in reply whereupon his wife asked me brightly what had been my worst experience in prison! My secretary, sensing that I was about to explode, either in tears or rage, managed to avert the conversation so there was no ugly scene. Later in the evening when the talk was over my hostess gave me a copy of the poem—a passage which has given me greater theological insight into my work than anything else I have seen written.

The next day one of my patients, Frank, a lovely North countryman, suddenly went off his legs—

became paralyzed from the waist down because the cancer in his kidney had invaded his spine. Over the next few days we explained to him that he would not walk again, and tried to help him grapple with the terrifying loss of his strength, independence and privacy. As I drove around the city and walked down the hospital corridors, I found myself saying again and again, "You wash the feet that will not walk tomorrow," and realized that this was my job, my calling. I, who have little patience with the demented and no love for tiny babies, have a special gift of warmth and understanding for those whose time is running out. I, who hate parties and find it nigh impossible to make small talk, know instinctively what to say and do for a gentle Manchester builder who is facing the humiliation of incontinence and the fear of death.

For everything, there is a season, for every task, someone is given the tools.

🖎

39

Good Friday and Easter Sunday Are One

Michael Leach

When I was in the seminary, an elderly priest told us, "Life is a series of Good Fridays with an occasional Easter thrown in just to keep us going."

We were young. "No!" we objected. "Life is an endless Easter with some Good Fridays thrown in to keep us on our toes!"

It wasn't until I was his age that I realized both sides are true.

When Vickie and I first met 42 years ago, I asked her, "What is your philosophy of life?"

She said without hesitation, "Life is for shit."

"How can you say that?" I said. "You're a happy, cheerful person."

"You see my eye," she said. Her right eye was scarred and cloudy, the color of a seashell. When she was fifteen months old Vickie fell on a glass Easter rabbit and was blinded. "When I was a little girl I walked with my face down so people wouldn't see how ugly I was. Sometimes people, even strangers, asked me embarrassing questions or made hurtful remarks. When the kids played games I was always the monster. I grew up imagining that everyone looked at me with disdain, as if the way I looked was my fault. I was a freak. Life was for shit. Thank God there was a heaven at the end."

I told her the truth: She was beautiful, in every way.

She knew I meant it. "What is your philosophy of life?" she asked.

"That heaven begins right here. We couldn't be further apart. Yet I walk around with sadness in my heart. And you walk around glowing. What gives?"

She was Good Friday with Easter in her heart. I was Easter with Good Friday on my back.

One year later we were married.

Forty-two years later, Vickie still believes that life is for shit, but she also knows that heaven does begin right here. I still believe that heaven begins right here but have also come to accept that life is for shit. We laugh a lot.

We have come to know that Easter and Good Friday are one.

"In this world you shall have tribulations," Jesus said, "but be of good cheer for I have overcome the world" (John 16:33).

Isn't that what Good Friday and Easter are all about?

Good Friday means you can nail beauty to a cross but you can't destroy it. Easter means you can bury love in a cave but it won't stay there. We begin to die the moment we're born but Jesus gives us new life the moment he dies. Jesus was our savior and the greatest teacher who ever lived. How wonderful to know that he rose from the dead, as he promised, to demonstrate that everything he taught about being loving and at peace was true.

"He departed from our sight," wrote St. Augustine, "so we might return to our heart and there find him. For he departed, and behold, he is here." Like E.T. who famously said, "I'll be right here," only for real!

Without Good Friday there can be no Easter. They are two sides of the same lost and found coin.

The old priest was right. The young seminarians were, too. Vickie and I taught each other one truth. We all forget Good Friday when love dissolves our pain. We each experience Easter when we fall and rise again, when we sin and discover, perhaps for the first time, that to God "our scarlet sins are whiter than snow" (Psalm 51:6), and every time a leaf blows by and we know that a new one is being born again.

Life is often cruel, but our Easter moments are more powerful than all the Good Fridays put together. Good Friday spurs us to behold what the poet Francis Thompson saw as "all the sweetness in the sad, the sadness in the sweet." Easter brings to mind the sweet lament of Cyrano de Bergerac: "There comes a moment, once—and God help those who pass that moment by!—when beauty stands looking into the soul with grave, sweet eyes that sicken at pretty words."

That moment is now. "Be still and know that I am God" (Psalm 46:10).

~

40

Good Friday: I Am Here

Greg Kandra

Sixty years ago, the psychiatrist Viktor Frankl wrote a best-selling book about his experiences as a prisoner in a concentration camp. *Man's Search for Meaning* is considered to be a classic about the worst nightmare of the last century. Frankl describes how men, women and children coped with the horrors of the camp— how they were able simply to survive, day after day, week after week.

At one point he tells the haunting story of a woman who knew she was going to die in just a few days. Despite that, he says, she was remarkably calm, even cheerful. One morning, Frankl approached this woman and asked her how she did it. How was she able to keep her spirits up? The woman told him that she had come to a deeper appreciation of spiritual things during her time in the camp.

Then, he writes:

> Pointing through the window of the hut, she said, "This tree here is the only friend I have in my loneliness." Through the window, she could see just one branch of a chestnut tree, and on the branch were two blossoms. "I often talk to this tree," she said to me . . . I asked her if the tree replied. "Yes." What did it say to her? She answered, "It said to me. 'I am here. I am here. I am life. Eternal life.'"

In that astonishing moment, Frankl touched on something profound. At the bleakest of moments, in even the darkest of places, we look for life. We want a promise of something better. We want to know that life goes on.

We crave hope.

Hope, however fleeting, was there in Auschwitz that morning. And, whether we realize it or not, hope is what has brought us together this afternoon.

In one sense, of course, we are remembering an event that seems hopeless—the agony and death of Jesus Christ. Today, in this liturgy, we re-read the story of His passion. We experience a deep and mournful absence—no consecration, no bells, no final blessing. The altar will be stripped.

For some people, it's still customary to turn off the radio, shut off the TV, draw the curtains . . . and pray. Some may light candles. Others may follow the Way of the Cross, or pray the Sorrowful Mysteries of the rosary.

The simple fact is: this can't be a day like any other. Scripture tells us that on the day Christ died, the world—literally—cracked open. The earth quaked. To this day, we cannot help but remember what was done for us. As the old spiritual tells us, it causes us to tremble.

But in the midst of all this, we do something remarkable.

We venerate the cross with a kiss.

I'm sure some outside our faith find it strange that we pay tribute to an instrument of death. But they don't see the cross the way we do. Maybe they should.

Maybe they should try to see that the cross was not an end, but a means to an end—the method God chose to remake the world. Maybe they should strive to see in the cross the beginning of our salvation. This is the wood of the cross, on which hung the savior of the world.

When the priest prays the Eucharistic Prayer for Reconciliation, which we hear so often during Lent, he invokes the cross powerfully, and poignantly. As the prayer puts it, Jesus "stretched out his arms between heaven and earth in the everlasting sign of Your covenant."

We are reminded today that it is a covenant that was sealed with nails, and splinters, and blood.

In the reading today from Isaiah, the prophet tells us about the suffering servant—foreshadowing Christ. Isaiah tells us: "He grew up like a sapling before him, like a shoot from the parched earth . . . it was our infirmities that he bore, our sufferings that he endured."

In Christ's cross, the wood we venerate and touch, we see part of the shoot from the parched earth. Nailed to this cross, He became one with it—and we are able to see this wood for what it truly is: a tree, like the one that prisoner saw, that holds out hope.

From within the four walls of our brokenness, behind the barbed wires of sin, we look out and look up —and we see this "tree" that symbolizes our salvation.

This is how we know we are saved. This is how we know how much God loves us.

This afternoon, the cross speaks to us. It speaks of the One who suffered and died upon it.

It speaks to us in consolation. And—yes—in hope.

And quietly, but persistently, it offers us the promise of something better, beyond the prison wall.

"I am here. I am here. I am life. I am Eternal life."

🖎

41

God Is a Loving Aunt

William J. Bausch

A little boy was afraid of the dark. One night his
mother told him to go out to the back porch and
bring her the broom. The little boy turned to the
mother and said, "Mama, I don't want to go out there.
It's dark."

The mother smiled reassuringly at her son.
"You don't have to be afraid of the dark, dear," she
explained. "Jesus is out there. He'll look after you and
protect you."

The little boy looked at the mother real hard and
asked, "Are you sure he's out there?

"Yes, I'm sure. He is everywhere, and he is always
ready to help you when you need him," she said.

The little boy thought about that for a minute and

then went to the back door and cracked it a little. "Jesus? If you're out there, would you please hand me the broom?"

In two weeks we will recall the death of Jesus, but today we are confronted with the death of Lazarus. It seems we're being asked to think about what we would prefer not to think about: death. And to ponder the little boy's question, "Jesus are you out there in the dark?" Really?

In answer, let me offer some suggestive images for you that indicate that Jesus is out there in the dark. Years ago, I had the opportunity to make a trip to Washington, D.C., with some friends. Part of our itinerary was to visit the Vietnam Memorial Wall. As you may know, the monument is a long black granite wall with thousands of names of those who lost their lives in the war. As I walked the grounds of the memorial, a couple of things stood out.

The first thing I noticed was the silence. As crowded as it was, there was a hush of reverence over the whole setting. The next thing that caught my eye was how different people approached the wall. Some were obviously just there as spectators. They could touch lots of names on the wall, pass them over quickly, and have no reaction whatsoever. To them, the names were just letters carved in a granite wall.

But to others, those names, or rather, this name, was a reason to pause, to cry. They moved very slowly as if approaching something sacred and then touched the name. Some wept, others were just still, lost in grief or reverie. Some stood quietly as they ran their fingers gently over the letters. Some even knelt. As I watched this ritual unfold, I couldn't help but wonder what the relationship was between the living person and the name: husband, son, father, brother, friend. It had to be something special or it would not have solicited such a reaction.

Of course, the answer is that to those who knew the person behind the name, it represents all the memories, the history, the personality and intimacy created between these two people. It is the depth of the relationship that makes the connection, the investment of life one person made in another person. It represents someone who made a difference to the one who knew that person.

And so too, Jesus. He said, "I know mine and mine know me." "I no longer call you servants but friends." So we are not anonymous to him. He runs his fingers over our names and claims us as his own before and after our deaths. That is our hope.

Another image. In a cemetery in Hannover, Germany, is a grave on which were placed huge slabs of granite and marble cemented together and fastened with heavy steel clasps. Why? Because it belonged to a woman who vehemently did not believe in the resurrection of the dead. So she directed in her will that her grave be made so secure that if there were a resurrection, it could not reach her. On the marker were inscribed these words: "This burial place must never be opened."

Ah, but in time, you see, what happened was that a tiny, infinitesimal seed, covered over by the stones, began to grow. Slowly it pushed its way through the soil. As it grew and its trunk enlarged, the great slabs of the grave were gradually shifted so that eventually the steel clasps were wrenched from their sockets and then, one day, there it was: the grave was exposed. A tiny seed had pushed aside those enormous stones.

Faith says that if nature can move huge stones, God can move the huge stone at Jesus' grave. And ours as well. Such is the force of God's love.

A third image. The luminous paintings of the great artist Renoir, are, as you know, aglow with life and light and color. He seemed to put light inside the people he painted. Remarkably, as you may also know, for the last twenty years or so of his life—his most productive years—Renoir was terribly crippled with arthritis. His hands were twisted and gnarled. His wrists, his arms, even his spine were ravaged by the disease. He couldn't even stand as he worked.

He had to sit as he painted and be shifted about in his chair by assistants. At times the pain was so great as he worked that beads of perspiration would stand out on his face. On one occasion, one of his students said to him, "Why do go on and torture yourself like this?" Renoir looked at the canvas he was working on and replied, "The pain passes, but the beauty remains."

That is the promise we have. "Untie him and set him free." That is to say, after the ravages of sickness and death, the beauty of love and eternity remain.

A fourth image. A celebrity of his time, playboy, wit, editor of the famous British publication *Punch*, Malcolm Muggeridge, much to the chagrin of his worldly friends, became a Christian. In fact, he became the worst kind: he became Catholic. He did so because he was inspired by the presence and work of Mother Teresa. Anyway, elderly when he converted, he wrote many lovely things, including these words of imagery:

As I approach my end, I find Jesus' outrageous claim ever more captivating and meaningful. Quite often, waking up in the night as the old do, I feel myself to be half out of my body, hovering between life and death, with eternity rising in the distance. I see my ancient carcass, prone between the sheets, stained and worn like a scrap of paper dropped in the gutter and, hovering over it, myself, like a butterfly released from its chrysalis stage and ready to fly away. Are caterpillars told of their impending resurrection? How in dying they will be transformed from poor earth crawlers into creatures of the air with exquisitely painted wings? If told, do they believe it?

I imagine the wise old caterpillars shaking their heads—no, it can't be; it's a fantasy. Yet in the limbo between living and dying, as the night clocks tick remorselessly on, and the black sky implacably shows not one single scratch of gray, I hear those words: "I am the resurrection" and then I feel myself to be carried along on a great tide of joy and peace.

Faith asks, "If caterpillars, why not we?"

A final image. A long time ago there lived a little boy whose parents had died. He was taken in by an aunt who raised him as her own child. Years later, after he had grown up and left his aunt, he received a letter from her. She was in terminal illness and, from the tone of her letter, he knew she was afraid of death. This man, whom she had raised and touched, wrote her a letter in which he said:

> It is now thirty-five years since I, a little boy of six, was left quite alone in the world. You sent me word that you would give me a home and be a mother to me. I've never forgotten the day when I made the long journey of ten miles to your house. I can still recall my disappointment when, instead of coming for me yourself, you sent your servant, Caesar, a dark man, to fetch me. I well remember my tears and my anxiety as, perched high on your horse and clinging tight to Caesar, I rode off to my new home. Night fell before we finished the journey and as it grew dark, I became even more afraid.
>
> "Do you think she'll go to bed before I get

there?" I asked Caesar anxiously. "Oh, no," said Caesar, "she'll sure to stay up for you. When we get out of these woods, you'll see her light shining in the window."

Presently, we did ride out into the clearing, and there was your light. I remember that you were waiting at the door; that you put your arms tight around me; that you lifted me—a tired, frightened little boy—down from the horse. You had a fire burning on the hearth; a hot supper waiting on the stove. After supper you took me to my new room. You heard me say my prayers. Then you sat with me until I fell asleep.

You probably realize why I am trying to recall this to your memory now. Very soon, God is going to send for you, and take you to a new home. I'm trying to tell you that you needn't be afraid of the summons or of the strange journey or of the dark messenger of death. God can be trusted. God can be trusted to do as much for you as you did for me so many years ago. At the end of the road you'll find love and a welcome waiting. And you'll be safe in God's care. I'm going to watch and pray for you until you're out of sight. And I shall wait for the day when I make the same journey myself and find you waiting at the end of the road to greet me.

Notice the symbols: Caesar, the dark figure, is death; the light at the end of the journey is Jesus, the light of the world; the house is the "many rooms" in the Father's house that Jesus promised; the supper is the heavenly banquet; God is the loving aunt. It's a homecoming story. It is gospel. It is hope. It is promise.

The little boy's question, "Jesus, are you out there?" must have been Lazarus' question. The Good News is that he was: for Lazarus, for you, and for me.

❧

42

It Is Finished in Beauty

Mary Lou Kownacki

I was typing a sentence condemning the brutal bomb-
ing of Iraqi children when she came into my study,
pulled my chair from the desk, took my hand, and
cried, "Hurry." We raced two blocks to an abandoned
house where a front yard had just been attacked and
overtaken by wild violets, by Johnny-jump-ups. We
stood in silence for three long minutes and cheered
the victory of beauty.

It is because I believe in the victory of beauty that
I have walked in the annual Good Friday Pilgrimage
for Peace sponsored by the Benedictine Sisters of Erie
since 1980. By putting one foot in front of the other
for seven miles, one can learn a lot about the journey
from evil to beauty, from despair to hope.

The pilgrimage begins in the inner city and winds its way to the monastery outside the city, stopping periodically to pray at stations where the body of Christ suffers today. We stop at the soup kitchen, where we are reminded that in the United States our city holds the dubious distinction of having the highest percentage of minority children living in poverty. There is a tavern that markets nude dancing, a symbol of how society encourages the exploitation and degradation of women.

Except for the prayers at the seven stations, the entire walk is done in silence. Parents with children, the lame in wheelchairs, the elderly, college students, and sisters—about 150 ordinary people—follow a simple wooden cross for the three-hour observance.

Once at the monastery, the pilgrims process into the chapel for the traditional Good Friday service with its readings, prayers, and adoration of the cross. After each pilgrim kisses the huge wooden cross and receives the broken body of Christ, the tabernacle door is closed, the altar is stripped, and silence returns. One could be left in despair, except that from the balcony comes the sound of a bell and two cantors sing over and over: "It is finished in beauty. It is finished in beauty." Then the final bell and the final silence.

Ah, yes, it is finished in beauty.

Tenacious wild violets erupting year after year no matter how many children are tortured worldwide is a glimmer of hope that God's plan for creation will triumph. Ordinary people participating in a seven-mile peace pilgrimage year after year despite growing lines at soup kitchens and escalating violence in our cities is a hope that death will not have the final word.

It is no mistake either, I believe, that Mary Magdalene first looked on the risen Jesus that early morning on the first day of the week, just after sunrise, and saw, of all things, a gardener. Our task is not about death, the empty tomb, and the empty shroud. It is about planting and sowing and caring for hope in whatever garden we find ourselves.

At the Easter Vigil in our monastery chapel, a sister dances the Alleluia banner down the center aisle, accompanied by hand bells and a congregation of hundreds singing "Alleluia."

Two dozen people process down the side aisles carrying flowers of every color and fragrance. In less than a minute an empty sanctuary is transformed into an overpowering garden of lilacs and tulips and hyacinths and daffodils. Hold fast to hope, the fragile flowers shout.

Ah, yes, it is finished in beauty.

🖝

43

Jesus Falls for the Third Time

Henri Nouwen

A man stumbles and falls to the ground. He is so weak and filled with pain that he cannot get back on his feet without help. As he lies there powerless, he reaches out and opens his hands, hoping that another hand will grasp his and help him to stand again. A hand waits for the touch of another hand. The human hand is so mysterious. It can create and destroy, caress and strike, make welcoming gestures and condemning signs; it can bless and curse, heal and wound, beg and give. A hand can become a threatening fist as well as a symbol of safety and protection. It can be most feared and most longed for.

One of the most life-giving images is that of human hands reaching out to each other, touching each other, interconnecting and merging into a sign of peace and reconciliation. In contrast, one of the most despairing images is that of a hand stretched open, waiting to be touched with care, while people walk heedlessly by. This is not only an image of the loneliness of the individual person, but of the loneliness of a divided humanity. The hand of the poor world reaches out to be touched by the hand of the rich world, but the preoccupations of the rich prevent them from seeing the poor, and humanity remains broken and fragmented.

When Jesus fell for the third time, he lived in his body all the loneliness of a despairing humanity. He could not get up again without help. But there was no one reaching out to him and offering him the support to stand again. Instead, his open hands were struck with a lash, and cruel hands pulled him back to a standing position. Jesus, God-made-human, falls so that we can bend over to him and show him our love and compassion, but we are too busy with other things even to notice. God, whose hands molded the universe, gave shape to Adam and Eve, touched every suffering person with tenderness, and who holds all things in love, became a human person with human hands asking for human hands. But those very hands were left open and pierced with nails.

Ever since I came to know God's hand—not as the powerful hand controlling the course of history, but as the powerless hand asking to be grasped by a caring human hand—I have been looking differently at my own hands. Gradually, I have come to see God's powerless hand reaching out to me from everywhere in the world, and, the clearer I see it, the closer these outstretched hands seem to be. The hands of the poor begging for food, the hands of the lonely calling for simple presence, the hands of the children asking to be lifted up and held, the hands of the sick hoping to be touched, the hands of the unskilled wanting to be trained—all these hands are the hands of the fallen Jesus waiting for others to come and give him their hand.

There is always in me the temptation to think about the begging hands of the people in Calcutta, Cairo, or New York, far, far away, and not to see the open hands reaching out right into my own living space. Every night I go to rest and look at my hands. And I have to ask them: "Did you reach out to one of the open hands around you and bring a little bit of peace, hope, courage, and confidence?" Somehow I sense that all human hands asking for help belong to the hands of our fallen humanity and that wherever we reach out and touch, we participate in the healing of the whole human race. Jesus falling and seeking help to get up again to fulfill his mission, opens up for us the possibility of touching God and all of humanity in every human hand and experiencing there the true grace of God's saving presence in our midst.

🖎

44

Did the Jesus Man Die?

Brian Doyle

In the small chapel on Bleak Friday, Dark Friday, Haunted Friday, Despair Friday, I watch a small girl gape as the massive priest strides up the aisle and then shockingly sprawls prone on the floor, his face pressed against the golden wood.

This *never* happens; Father Jim always bows deeply and then strides briskly up and around the altar like he built it, which actually he did, being a terrific carpenter.

The chapel shivers with silence.

Is he okay, mama? Is he hurt? Is he sleeping?

We hid as it were our faces from him; he was despised, and we esteemed him not.

This girl is maybe three years old, I think; old

enough to be riveted, not old enough to be cynical about the stunning theater of the moment.

He was wounded for our transgressions, he was bruised for our iniquities: with his stripes we are healed.

Whereas her brother is sound asleep on his mother's sparrow shoulder, his sweet drool marking a line like a river on the green meadow of her coat.

Of all the people on earth, of all the people who ever were and are and will be, how astounding, how incredible, that the one appointed to bear all ills, to carry all wounds, to stand for all, to be sacrificed and resurrected, to be both king of pain and prince of light, should be a thin Arab woodworker, a most devout and committed Jew? Do we gape in amazement at this totally odd detail as much as we should? Do we remember how wild it is that the One among us was not strong or wealthy, famous or charming, beautiful or honored, but a footloose vagrant on Roman roads, troublesome and strange? Of all the people in all the world, *that* guy? That's the last guy you would ever imagine, the last kid picked, the homeless guy with dirty feet.

Could that be the point, the genius, the secret?

Let us therefore come boldly unto the throne of

grace, that we may obtain mercy, and find grace to help in time of need.

Amen to that, kid, I whisper to the gangly teenager reading Paul's letter aloud. Amen to *that*. The boy then opens his mouth and begins to sing in a baritone thicker than he is.

The *naked* altar, the empty yawning candleholders, the elderly priests sitting together in the rear of the chapel, the shy students, the graying neighbors.

To this end was I born, and for this cause came I into the world, that I should bear witness unto the truth. Everyone that is of the truth heareth my voice.

Even unto a small chapel on a sandy bluff over a broad river thousands of years later His voice washing over a small girl with pink Sesame Street mittens; the left with Bert's face and the right with Ernie's. On her hat, crumpled on the seat she never sits in once, is the sweet bright face of Elmo; all I can see is an eye, but I would recognize that joyous eye anywhere.

What I have written I have written.

The sigh and rustle of the congregation like a wave in the sea. The crackle of their knees as they sink to the floor as He hangs on the cross. His last instructions: Behold thy son! Behold thy mother! And the penultimate line that always makes me cry, in my dark corner, where the sight lines are such that I can see the whole trial and murder but no one can see me crying: *I thirst.*

Me too, man, I whisper. Me too. For the sepulcher is nigh at hand.

The small girl gapes again when Father Jim sings the adoration aloud, her mouth falls open just like a kid in the movies who sees something spectacular, and then when a student in the back of the chapel stands up and sings back to Father Jim she yanks her dad's hand like a chain and he picks her up and her face beams over his shoulder like a sudden apple.

Sometimes it causes me to tremble, tremble, tremble, sings the choir.

Me too, you beautiful tall singing children, I whisper. Me too.

The shuffle of socks against the golden wood of the chapel floor. The boy in brilliant red sneakers kneeling to kiss the cross. The girl who holds her hair back with one hand as she kisses the cross. The boy who hugs it like a lover. The priest resting his forehead against it. The old man who touches it with his cane. The star basketball player who folds himself down and down to touch it with the huge nets of his hands. The shaking man whose touch is taps. The shiver of silence as the priest lifts his hands in blessing but then walks away to the side, the one day all year when he will not walk triumphantly down the aisle like a hero parting a sea of smiles. The small girl puzzled as her mom and dad and drooling brother turn to leave.

Did he die, mama? Did the Jesus man die?

Yes, honey. He died.

But he gets born again? When does he get born again?

Tomorrow, says her mother, a freighted word I catch just as I follow them through the immense walnut doors of the chapel into the shocking light, the last thing you ever expect on Good Friday is to emerge from the haunted darkness into such a crisp redolent spring afternoon, this nails me every year, no matter how wet a winter it's been this day without fail is the most crystalline miracle imaginable, how ironic or momentous is that?, but as I turn to shuffle west I hear the father say faintly, almost under his breath,

Today.

Maybe he meant something else altogether, maybe he was starting to say something about prospective dinner plans or what crucial basketball game was on television or what cool playground they could stop at on the way home, but I don't think so. I think the father, young as he was, and he looked to be about thirty, said the truth; we are all born again today. You and me and the kid with the mittens and the thin Arab woodworker. Today.

❧

45

Crucifixion and Resurrection

Mary Christine Athans

Mary speaks:

I could not believe how exhausted I was. If it were not for Mary Magdalene and the other women, I might have collapsed along the way. They practically carried me to Golgotha along the cobblestone streets. I had stayed at the foot of the cross with John, my sister, and Mary Magdalene—but shortly before Jesus died, the soldiers hurried us up the hill. We only saw from afar when they pierced his side. It was as if my heart were pierced, too.

We watched as they took Jesus' body down from the cross. It had all been so brutal! I was very grateful to John for being there to the end. Joseph of Arimathea had arranged with Pilate to remove the body and bury it. Nico-

demus helped Joseph by bringing burial cloths as well as myrrh and aloes, according to custom. They were able to lay Jesus in a garden tomb nearby (Jn 20:38–42). It had to be hastily done before sundown, when Passover and Shabbat would begin.

After they removed Jesus' body, we walked slowly to the upper room where we would celebrate Shabbat and Passover. They don't often fall on the same day. Mary Magdalene was in tears, but I leaned on her the whole way. They let me rest while the final preparations for Passover were completed. Everything seemed so somber. There was no joy this year. They asked me to bless the candles, which had to be lit before sunset.

Before creation there was darkness, so after lighting the candles, I covered my eyes and beckoned the warmth of the Shabbat with my hands while saying the prayer: Ba-ruch a-ta A do-nai E-lo-hei-nu, me-lach ha o-lom, a-sher ki-de-sha-nu be-mitz-vo-tav ve-tsi va-nu le-had-lik neir shel Shab-bat ve-shel Yom tov (Blessed are you, O Lord our God, Ruler of the Universe, who has sanctified our lives through your commandments, commanding us to kindle the Shabbat and the festival lights). Even from before the time of the Maccabees, our people have lit lights on Shabbat. To illumine a Jewish home with lights on Shabbat represents creation as well as a foretaste of the in-

effable bliss of life eternal. This night more than any other, I prayed that my dear son, Jesus, would taste such bliss.

Here I was in Jerusalem for Passover, as I had been with Joseph and Jesus and so many family members over the years. I remember so well the time Jesus got lost when he was only twelve and gave us a scare. It was such a relief to find him in the Temple where he was asking questions of the great sage Hillel and some of the other sages who seemed to admire the wisdom of our young son. But I never understood Jesus' answer to me: "Did you not know I must be in my Father's house?" (Lk 2:49). Many things he said over the years were so simple and full of truth; others were so mysterious. Yet, he was obedient to us, and grew in wisdom, age, and divine favor. Hard to believe that was almost twenty years ago.

The meal was subdued—and I was tired. Some of the men had brought home the lamb, which had been sacrificed that afternoon in the Temple. As we ate, we recounted the story of the Exodus, how God had freed us from Egypt, allowed us to escape through the Red Sea, fed us manna in the desert. It was always a time of zikaron. Somehow, in the telling of the story and doing the ritual, the past becomes present in our lives. We were slaves in Egypt and now we are free. So, too, Jesus is now free.

Another favorite song of mine is the Dayeinu (It

would have been enough). Any of these gifts that God had given us "would have been enough!" Yet, God continued to bless us and shower us with gifts. How could we repay him? Even in our sorrow we sang, sometimes through our tears, Dayeinu!—It would have been enough!

Had God brought us out of Egypt and not
divided the sea for us, *Dayeinu!*

Had God divided the sea for us and not permitted us to cross the dry land, *Dayeinu!*

Had God permitted us to cross the sea on dry
land and not sustained us for forty years in
the desert, *Dayeinu!*

Had God sustained us . . . in the desert and not
fed us with manna, *Dayeinu!*

Had God fed us with manna and not given us
the Sabbath, *Dayeinu!*

Had God given us the Sabbath but not brought
us to Mount Sinai, *Dayeinu!*

Had God brought us to Mount Sinai but not
given us the Torah, *Dayeinu!*

Had God given us the Torah and not led us to
the land of Israel, *Dayeinu!*

Had God led us to the land of Israel and not
built for us the Temple, *Dayeinu!*

Had God built for us the Temple but not sent us

the prophets of truth, *Dayeinu!*
Had God sent us the prophets of truth and not
made us a holy people, *Dayeinu!*

Somehow, on this special night, I could not stop there.
In my heart I continued to sing:

Had God given me such a beautiful baby but not
let us escape to Egypt, *it would have been*
enough!

Had God let us escape to Egypt, but not find
our way back to Galilee, *it would have been*
enough!

Had God let us come back to Galilee, but not
let us find him in the Temple, *it would have*
been enough!

Had God let us find him in the Temple, but not
allow him to return with us to Nazareth, *it*
would have been enough!

Had God let him return with us to Nazareth,
but not let him begin his ministry of
preaching, *it would have been enough!*

Had God let him begin his ministry of preaching, but not heal the sick and feed the
hungry, *it would have been enough!*

Had God allowed him to heal the sick and feed
the hungry, but not let him give his life for
us, *it would have been enough!*

*How could I ever thank God for the gift of Jesus? Even
holding him in my arms that first night would have been
enough. Yet God gave him to me for a lifetime—too short
a life, but a blessed life! I knew from the beginning that it
was a mystery. I also believed in God's faithful love—and
that God's love would be there to the end. I needed to continue to trust. The Sabbath lights are still lit—and they
are a foretaste of Life Eternal!*

*Finally, the tiredness descended upon everyone, and
people started to leave. John, Peter, James, and the others
all came to comfort me. I knew I had to be strong for them.
They were so heartbroken, and some of them, like Peter,
felt so guilty. I fear he believed he could never do enough
repentance—t'shuvah. He cried through the whole meal. I
told them to try to sleep—we needed a Shabbat of rest and
a time to reflect. After Shabbat we would come together
again and look to the future.*

*That Passover/Shabbat day was very quiet. Although
we could hear others celebrating, we had no desire to go
anywhere. I was very grateful to have a small room in the
home of a friend of Mary Magdalene's who was generous*

enough to let us stay with her. Mary was so attentive to me and yet anguished herself. She loved Jesus so much. But I really needed to be alone.

At the end of the Shabbat we all gathered again for Havdalah—when we can finally see three stars in the sky. Jesus used to love Havdalah! He used to run outside with the other children when he was little and count the stars. The prayers of this wonderful ancient service which marks the outgoing of the Sabbath, spoke to us all: "Behold, God is my salvation; I will trust and will not be afraid." That psalm begins: "God is our refuge and strength, a very present help in trouble. Therefore we will not fear, though the earth be moved, and though the mountains be carried into the midst of the seas." Although our world had turned upside down, God would be our refuge and our strength.

The cup of wine was raised and we said Baruch a-tah A-don-ai, Eloheinu mel-ach ha-olam, bor-ay p'ree ha-gafen (Blessed are you, O Lord our God, Ruler of the Universe, who has given us the fruit of the vine). After all said Amen, we each had a sip. Then the spice box was raised to remind us of the sweetness of the Sabbath, and we said, "Blessed are you, O Lord our God, Ruler of the Universe, who creates different kinds of spices." And after an Amen, we passed the beautiful box of spices around for all to sniff—to carry some of the sweetness of the Sabbath into the week ahead. I was probably not the only one who thought instead of the spices that would be brought to the tomb tomorrow to give my Jesus a proper burial.

Last, now that Shabbat was over we could kindle lights again—the special braided Havdalah candle with the two wicks. We prayed, "Blessed are you, O Lord our God, Ruler of the Universe, who created the lights of the fire!" We put our hands forward so we could make use of the fire. Light was the first thing created by God, and God also gave us fire to warm ourselves. On this painful night we needed light and warmth. The final benediction reminded us of the distinction between the Sabbath and the six days ahead. We needed God to help us survive the pain and sorrow of these days. What would they bring?

Once again, the group dispersed. The women started to busy themselves preparing spices and oil to take to the tomb in the morning. I went back to my little room, grateful for the solitude. I prayed wordlessly—remembering the joy of his smile and his laugh. It seemed so unreal that he was gone. I knew that there would be a resurrection of the body and that we would be together in the end times, but I just never thought he would leave us so young.

As I sat there with my eyes closed, I felt a gentle hand on my shoulder. That was something Jesus often did when he came in from the workshop—when I was engrossed in thought and prayer as I was sewing. I must be imagining it—remembering how he would thoughtfully bring me a cup of water and gently touch my hand. Then I heard him say, "Ema—mother." I opened my eyes and turned. He was there with a certain radiant glow! It was almost as it had been those many years ago when the mysterious figure appeared to tell me I would be his mother! But I was not afraid this time. He helped me stand up. Was I dreaming? I buried my head in his shoulder, and my tears overflowed. It was almost as it had been when I ran to Elizabeth and wept with pent up pain and joy—but this time it was joy overflowing with a depth of gratitude I could never have imagined. It was a joy born out of pain.

He held me gently and spoke softly. Somehow he had to suffer in order to enter into his glory. That's what Simeon had meant that day in the Temple so long ago. His mission would become clear in the days ahead. For tonight, all I knew was joy and gratitude. I recalled the night that he was born, and I could still think of no better prayer to offer with an overflowing heart to a loving and faithful God. I paused for moment and said, "Jesus, do you think we should say a She-he-chee-ya-nu?" He nodded and smiled, and together we prayed:

Ba-ruch a-tah A-don-ai

All Shall Be Well

E-lo-hei-nu, me-lech ha-o-lam,
She-he-chee-ya-nu ve-ki-ye-ma-nu
ve-hi-gi-a-nu- la-ze-man ha-zeh.

Blessed are You, O Lord our God,
Ruler of the Universe,
who has given us life,
and sustained us,
and brought us to this very special moment.

46

The Glad Surprise

Howard Thurman

There is ever something compelling and exhilarating about the glad surprise. The emphasis is upon *glad*. There are surprises that are shocking, startling, frightening, and bewildering. But the glad surprise is something different from all of these. It carries with it the element of elation, of life, of something over and beyond the surprise itself. The experience itself comes at many levels: the simple joy that comes when one discovers that the balance in the bank is larger than the personal record indicated—and there is no error in accounting; the realization that one does not have his doorkey—the hour is late and everyone is asleep—but someone very thoughtfully left the latch off, "just in case"; the dreaded meeting in a conference to work out some problems of misunderstanding, and things are adjusted without the emotional lacerations anticipated; the report from the doctor's examination that all is well, when one was sure that the physical picture was very serious indeed. All of these surprises are glad!

There is a deeper meaning in the concept of the glad surprise. This meaning has to do with the very ground and foundation of hope about the nature of life itself. The manifestation of this quality in the world about us can best be witnessed in the coming of spring. It is ever a new thing, a glad surprise, the stirring of Life at the end of winter. One day there seems to be no sign of life and then almost overnight, swelling buds, delicate blooms, blades of grass, bugs, insects—an entire world of newness everywhere. It is the glad surprise at the end of winter. Often the same experience comes at the end of a long tunnel of tragedy and tribulation. It is as if a man stumbling in the darkness, having lost his way, finds that the spot at which he falls is the foot of a stairway that leads from darkness into light. Such is the glad surprise. This is what Easter means in the experience of the race. This is the resurrection! It is the announcement that life cannot ultimately be conquered by death, that there is no road that is at last swallowed up in an ultimate darkness, that there is strength added when the labors increase, that multiplied peace matches multiplied trials, that life is bottomed by the glad surprise. Take courage, therefore:

> When we have exhausted our store of endurance,
> When our strength has failed ere the day is half
>   done,
> When we reach the end of our hoarded resources,
> Our Father's full giving is only begun.

🖎

47

Tell Them

Edwina Gateley

Breaking through the powers of darkness
bursting from the stifling tomb
he slipped into the graveyard garden
to smell the blossomed air.

Tell them, Mary, Jesus said,
that I have journeyed far
into the darkest deeps I've been
in nights without a star.

Tell them, Mary, Jesus said,
that fear will flee my light
that though the ground will tremble
and despair will stalk the earth

I hold them firmly by the hand
through terror to new birth.

Tell them, Mary, Jesus said,
the globe and all that's made
is clasped to God's great bosom
they must not be afraid
for though they fall and die, he said,
and the black earth wrap them tight
they will know the warmth
of God's healing hands
in the early morning light.

Tell them, Mary, Jesus said,
smelling the blossomed air,
tell my people to rise with me
to heal the Earth's despair.

🖎

48

Very Early Sunday Morning

William J. O'Malley, SJ

Mary Magdalene scurried along the street at the earliest hint of dawn. She had made certain she could distinguish a white from a black thread, that the Sabbath and feast were clearly over and the work week had begun again. On one hip she carried a jug of water with a clean towel looped through the handle, on the other a flask with the funeral spices ready mixed. Only the most dedicated shopkeepers were already setting up their stalls along the street. The sun wasn't yet high enough to warm away the night chill.

She came up to the Damascus Gate and saw the Roman guards at their posts, yawning and scratching. The final night watch went from three to six. They made no move to stop her. The orders had been to stop "any *men*." And their relief was already overdue. When you've got a job, why go looking for work?

But the sight of them made her stop in her tracks.

Fool, she thought to herself. The stone. That evening it had taken three men.

She almost went back for help, but little chance any of the men could be lured out where anyone at all might recognize them. No one could tell one woman from another unless she were a hag or a whore.

I can sit, she thought. And wait. And pray. And he won't be alone.

She passed through the gate. The guards were too sleep-needful to be rude. She picked her way down the long slope into the overgrown area where the tombs stood, and she pushed her way through the brush to the path in front of the rich man's grotto.

Suddenly, she was again struck still, staring. Open-mouthed. The flask slipped from her grip, and the crockery jug shattered on the rocks.

The round stone lay flat on the ground, cracked in two. The tomb gaped open.

Oh, no! Someone's taken him.

She turned on her heel, rucked up her skirts and began to run back up the slope to the gate. The guards stopped their fiddling and gaped, ready to jump whatever drunk fool from the graveyard was after her, but no one came. As she ran along the cobbles, merchants stopped their fussing, too, and wondered what could have gotten into this madwoman. Women don't run.

Mary burst through the street door of the hiding place, up the stairs, and hammered on the barred door of the room where the men were hiding. Young John opened it only a few inches, one eye peering out.

"Are they after you?" he choked.

"No, you fool. Get Simon! They've taken him away. Out of the tomb!" And she turned down the stairs again. She waited at the bottom for what seemed forever while John roused Simon Peter, who had said not a word to anyone since it happened.

"Come!" Mary shouted. "We have to find where they put him!"

The three ran along the street like fugitives. As they hurtled through the gates, the squad of guards still waiting their relief sprang up and hollered, "Halt! *Stop!*"

The three disciples stopped, poised to run again. "They've robbed the grave!" John shouted, and the three started away. Two guards set off in their wake. "Come back here!"

The woman and two men found the path through

the brush and stood in front of the gaping hole. The two soldiers caught up with them, all five breathless. Uncertain what to do. What might be lurking inside a grave.

"By the gods," said one guard. "No way! I swear, no one came out of here last night!"

The older one pushed forward. "There was that god-awful storm. Great thunderclaps. They might have slipped by, no? And the noise? That young one was crapping his pants. Lightning couldn't have done that to that stone. Could it?"

John picked up his courage, bent down, and peered into the darkness. In the shadows, he saw the winding sheet in a heap. The cave empty. He backed out and gestured Peter in.

Peter stooped and pushed into the shallow cave. He saw the bloodstained shroud on the floor beneath the ledge. Oddly, the kerchief from the corpse's face was on the ledge, but folded carefully by itself, neatly. Who would steal a body and leave the grave cloths? What Jew would dare *tref*, touching a body so long dead?

The two backed into the gathering light. "Lightning didn't take his body," Simon said.

The older guard looked in and backed out, sputtering. "I'll cover the gate," he said to the other. "Go tell them back at the praetorium." And both ran up the incline to the gate.

John brushed past the astonished Peter, and put his head into the opening again, looking around in the dim emptiness. He smiled and spoke so softly the others failed to hear him. "He did it." Then he shook his head. Wishful thinking. The body was simply gone. But how? Why?

The two men moved disconsolately out of the gloom. Mary stood with tears brimming in her eyes and dribbling down her cheeks. She looked with brief hope at the others. Her fist went to her mouth as she realized the men were as baffled as she was.

Peter and John trudged up the long slope to the gate, leaving Mary standing outside the tomb, like Lot's wife. Her mind was utterly blank. There had to be an answer.

She stooped and for the first time actually looked into the empty cavern herself.

But it wasn't empty. Or her brain was fevered.

There were two *presences*. Radiances. Hovering over the ledge, one at the head, the other at the foot. One spoke. "Woman," it said, in a voice like music. "Why are you crying?"

"Our teacher," she faltered. "They've taken him away. I don't know where to find him."

Bewildered, she turned to leave. But a man stood in her way. "Woman," he said, exactly like the angel, "Why are you crying?"

She twitched in surprise. The caretaker. "Oh, *sir!*" she said. "If you took him . . . please! Tell me where. So I can bring him back. I *have* to bring him back!"

The man said, very softly, "Mary."

Magdalene's fist struck her heart. And she knew. "Teacher," she breathed and fell to her knees, grasping his legs.

He caught her elbows, lifting her to her feet again. "Don't cling. I'm here. I'm here for a time. At least like this. So. Go to my brothers, yes? And Peter. Tell them."

And, suddenly, the solidity of him was simply no longer there.

Once again, in a delirium of doubt and disbelief and utter certainty, she ran up the hill, past the astonished guards, through the gate and onto the long cobbled street to the house where the apostles were hiding. She slammed through the door, grabbed her skirts to run up the stairs. She hammered on the door. And hammered.

"I've seen him!" she cried. "I've seen him! He's *alive* again!"

Again, John opened the door carefully, his face agape. They were all sitting around the upper room, dumbfounded as she rattled on wildly about the shining presences, the voice, the caretaker, the feel of his legs.

And of course they didn't believe a word of it. Hysterical woman.

In the late afternoon, the people from downstairs had left them wine and food, and the men had barred the door behind them. The Magdalene, sputtering and hammering at their chests and shoulders because they refused to believe her nonsense, went down with them . . .

When she had first come back, she had stirred a tornado of responses, cynical, scowling, half-hopeful, ultimately derisive. She'd been possessed once, hadn't she? Seven devils? Unstable. Yes, he *had* spoken of it. Rising again. But later. Much, much later. Centuries.

And half the rabbis said even that was a delusion. Yes, they'd believed it themselves. Awhile. Simply because they'd so desperately wanted to believe it. To believe that life could be larger than the day-after-day frustrations and resentments and predictable defeats. Like this.

They'd left home for him. Risked everything that meant anything. Even their faith.

Then again. What if—what if impossibly—it were true? They'd run. They'd left him alone. With the venomous priests and the brutal police. How could they dare face him if this was true?

But if he had *really* been who they'd begun to believe he was, he *could* have saved himself. Surely. He'd done it before. At the very beginning, when the Nazareth men were ready to hurl him off the cliff. He just walked right through them. Like Moses through the Red Sea. And last winter, on Solomon's porch, when the locals had picked up rocks to stone him because they thought he was making himself into God. And they tried to arrest him? He just walked away like a priest from beggars.

He could have done it in the garden. When they ran. But he'd *told* them to. Practically.

Now some madmen had taken his corpse. What possible brainsick reason? The last thing the priests would have tolerated. Not the Romans. Some perverted sect? Had Jesus infuriated anyone else? Too many to choose from.

And round and round and forward and backwards and up and down until they'd exhausted all arguments, all tolerance, all hope for meaning. One another. Finally, they all eased back into the dark torpor they'd sulked in for days.

Later, not one of them—not a single one—could find words for what happened next.

From out of nowhere, there he *was*.

But radiant. Hard to look straight at. His gown woven of light.

There was no way to test it. Or need to. He was as real as you know bread and wine are real, without need to taste or touch them.

He said, very quietly, "Peace." He held out his wrists. They saw the holes, healed. He parted the gown at the neck and showed them the scar over his heart. They could hardly breathe.

"Now," he said. "The mission is yours. As the Father sent me to you, I send you. My Spirit is now breathed into you. Take it out to the whole world. Forgive those who regret and repent. Those who refuse you, refuse love."

Then he went to Peter, crouching disconsolately by the wall, terrified, simply unable to look up. Jesus reached down, took his elbows as he had Magdalene, and raised him up. He looked into Peter's frightened, tear-filled eyes. Then he wrapped his arms around him. Tight.

And then he was gone. Just not there anymore. And yet . . .

That same evening, a couple of hours before dark, Cleophas, Jesus' uncle, and his wife, Mary, who'd been at the cross, were making their way unhappily toward Emmaus, a town seven miles northwest of the city at the end of Ayalon Valley. Two hours' walk. An overnight stopover on their long journey back to Galilee. Get a leg of the journey out of the way. More importantly, get away from the cauldron of Jerusalem and its destruction of their profoundest hopes. The open road was more dangerous after dark, but it was a place to breathe and to unburden themselves of the shattered illusions they dared not broach in the city, even in whispers.

Arguing, as spouses sometimes do. Mary was cautiously exuberant, hoping the news was true—and more important, rerooting their hopes. The tomb was definitely empty. Even stubborn Simon admitted that. And, say what you want about the Magdala woman, she was there when they killed him. Mary had been there herself. And Magdalene had also seen him. Well, then? "And don't give me that 'she's only a woman!' She was there before any man!"

Cleophas was sourly convinced it was all over. So they had almost tired of snapping at one another, re-hashing "And what will we do now?"

Suddenly, she put her hand on her husband's arm to silence him. "Someone's back there," she whispered. They stopped, and Cleophas moved in front of his wife and lifted his stout staff at an angle in front of them, ready.

The stranger was a big man, and the couple tensed. But he was alone. The sky was darkening. The village inn was only a bit up the road. But neither of them could outrun him.

The man raised his hand. "Hello!" he hollered. "I'm alone. Don't be afraid. I mean you no harm. May I join you?"

He approached slowly, hands empty in the air. The couple was stiffly wary, angling their eyes around him in case there were others.

"My name is Cleophas," the man volunteered, cautiously. "This is my wife, Mary."

"Are you on your way north?"

"Eventually."

"Thank you for letting me walk with you," the

stranger said. "It gets lonely."

"Yes," the woman murmured, still watchful, uncomfortable.

"Forgive me. In the silence I couldn't help hearing. You seemed to be mourning. I hope I'm not interfering."

Cleophas replied, "This weekend. The teacher. We had such hopes." He fought the tears.

"Teacher?" the stranger echoed.

"Jesus. The Nazarene. It was heartbreaking."

"Heartbreaking?"

"Weren't you coming from Jerusalem?"

"And thereabouts."

"And you didn't hear about the clamor last weekend? When he arrived. And the uproar at his trial when all the fools wanted him crucified?"

"Tell me."

"We thought. . . ," Mary said.

"We thought he was the One," Cleophas interrupted, "you know? The Messiah. He did wondrous things. Curing people. And teaching kindness. Forgiveness. No matter what. But...but then he... pushed things too far. They say he did. They say he claimed he was...he was equal to God. Or something like that."

"That's why they killed him," Mary said. "Then they told the Romans he wanted to be made king. The priests made that up. Because of the Messiah being...well, like David. But he wasn't like that at all. But the Romans didn't want trouble. So they crucified him. That gentle, kind man. They nailed his hands and feet, and. . ," she began to choke on her tears.

"She was there," Cleophas said, and put his arm around her shoulders. "Such hopes. But the Messiah's not supposed to be...to be degraded like that...not treated like a dog. The Holy One would never allow that."

"Why not?" the stranger asked.

The man and wife stopped and stood, unsure again. "Are you a Jew?" Cleophas asked.

"Of course," the big stranger smiled.

"Then you've been taught. The holy books say Elijah would come. That was John the Baptist. Then the Messiah would come, like Moses, and lead us out of bondage again. And like David, he'd make us a people again. Make all things right again."

"Like this Nazarene," the stranger said, "just healing, forgiving, bringing only peace."

"Yes." Mary's tears were running freely now, and her husband's were brimming.

"The holy books," the big stranger said. "You remember Job?"

"Of course," Cleophas replied, a bit insulted.

"But you don't remember, early on? Before Job's friends confused him? When he said, 'Naked came I out of my mother's womb, and naked shall I return thither. The Lord gave, and the Lord hath taken away; blessed be the name of the Lord.' You were willing to take the good parts—the healing, the forgiveness. But not the pain, not the cost of loving."

"But…"

"You've let the priests push aside the prophets. They goad you with fear onto the right road and then they brighten it with the promise to take away all pain, all sorrow. Instead of helping you make sense of it." He smiled at Mary. "Do you have children?"

"Four," she said.

"Were any of their births joyous?"

She hesitated. "When it was over."

"Exactly! Suffering, then joy. Neither one would have any meaning without the other."

They began to walk again, more slowly now. And the stranger led them through the Scriptures, quoting passage after passage that showed them how shallow and one-sided their ideas of the Messiah had been.

He reminded them of Isaiah's Messiah, "'There was nothing appealing about him, nothing to call for a second look. Despised, useless, a man who knew pain like his shadow. Shunned, reviled, dirt. But it was *our* pains he carried, *our* burdens, *our* disfigurements, whatever is wrong with *us*.'"

The husband and wife listened, fumbling to take it in as he went on and on. "'He was beaten, tortured, but he didn't say a word. A lamb to the slaughter. Silent. They trampled justice to take him away. Who could have guessed what was really happening? Slain for the sins of my people, buried with the wicked, even though he'd never harmed a soul or said one untrue word.'"

He quoted Zechariah as knowingly as if he had written it himself: "'Oh, then I'll rain down a torrent of grace and peace on the house of David and all in Jerusalem. They'll look at Me whom they pierced. They will mourn for Him as for an only child.' As you were mourning."

Without realizing, they had walked into the village, where the oil lamps were beginning to puncture the darkness. The inn was just ahead.

"Well, then," the stranger smiled broadly again. "Here we are. I'll be going on."

"It's late," Mary said, a hint of concern in her voice. "It's too dangerous on the road in the dark. By yourself."

"Have you eaten?" Cleophas asked.

"Not in some time," the stranger answered.

"Then come in for a bite," Mary urged. "And stay the night. Not expensive. We checked. And if you haven't enough…"

So they went in and found places in the noisy tavern. When their food came, the stranger reached bread from the basket and said: *"Barukh attah Adonai Elohenu Melek . . .* Blessed are you, O Lord our God, King of Ages, who brings forth bread from earth." He looked at his two friends, and tore the bread in half, handing them the pieces, taking none himself.

They had followed him a very long time. At the wedding he had transformed water into wine. Out in the stony wilderness, he had—somehow—fed thousands with no more than a couple of loaves. They had heard the Twelve whispering about his mystical farewell meal with them the night before that horrible day.

And at that instant, they knew him. In the breaking of the bread.

Then, suddenly, he was no longer there. And yet . . .

Thomas the Twin had not been with them that first time. When they told him they'd seen Jesus, his first reaction was fury. A joke like that was heartless. Obscene. The more they tried to persuade him, the stronger his resistance grew. They were all as crazy as the devil-woman. "Just stop it!" he finally shouted. "When I put my finger into his wrists and my hand into his chest, then I'll believe the rotten lot of you!"

A week later, Jesus met Thomas's challenge.

They were huddled together in the upper room, all eleven of the ones still faithful. Each in his own way. There'd been no news of a pogrom from the Temple. On the other hand, there'd been no news of a reprieve and no end of rumors.

Then, from nowhere, Jesus stood there among them. Solid, impenetrable, real. Even if the door to the stairs was barred. Right next to where Thomas hunched at the end of a couch.

"Shalom," he said softly. "I missed you, Thomas."

Thomas shuddered. Terrified. Confounded. "Oh, my God!" he gasped.

Jesus hugged the poor man in his big arms and stroked his back. "Oh, Thomas," he said. "I know it's hard." Then he held him at arm's length, let him go.

He held out his wrists. "Put your finger into the scars, Thomas. Don't ever be afraid again."

But Thomas couldn't. And there was no need to.

Now Jesus did many other signs in the presence of his disciples, which are not written in this book. But these are written so that you may come to believe that Jesus is the Messiah, the Son of God, and that through believing you may have life in his name. (Jn 20:30-31)

49

The Resurrection of the Nonviolent Jesus

John Dear

On the first morning of the week, Mary Magdalene arrives at the tomb to anoint Jesus' body—only to find an empty tomb. The story of Lazarus has come full circle. The One who called humanity from its tomb and died a subversive's death—he himself rose to new life. Once again an empty tomb.

She's puzzled—what foul play is this?—and she lingers and weeps.

"Woman, why are you weeping? Whom are you looking for?" It's the voice of Jesus, whom she mistakes for the gardener.

At hearing him utter her name, she recognizes

who he is—another literary gem pointing to a spiritual truth. She would embrace him but he sends her on a mission. "Go and tell my brothers that I am risen."

Ladies and gents, meet Mary Magdalene, the first apostle of the resurrection. Jesus sends her off to proclaim it to those still entombed in the culture of death. The shame his culture heaps on women is no deterrent to Jesus. He grants her the honor now of liberating the entombed.

That evening Jesus appears to the community locked away in hiding. "Peace be with you" are his first words. Then after showing them the wounds of his crucifixion, he says again: "Peace be with you." John is pressing a point—a startling point, so he presses it obliquely. He's telling us that the peace Jesus offers is contingent on his wounds. Resurrection peace comes by way of nonviolently resisting the culture of death. Shortly put, by risking the cross. More startling yet, he passes the mantle on. "As the Father sent me, so I send you." And he breathes on them—"Receive the Holy Spirit"—and then confers on them soaring authority. "Those whom you forgive, are forgiven. Those you hold in community are retained." An authority vastly different than that of emperors and rulers. Here

Jesus confers authority to reconcile. With these words he sends them into the chaotic world of violence to build communities of nonviolence, a mission passed down through the ages to ourselves.

Now we are to live together in the spirit of *agape* and peace, as servants of life, as proclaimers of the resurrection and all its social, economic, and political implications, understanding full well that Jesus' resurrection was illegal, knowing that it portends the undoing of empire because it robs the state of its only intimidation—the threat of death. We are to trust and proclaim. Death has no more sway; it is struck from empire's hands. It is not something to fear but to defy.

Little do we realize: the resurrection of Jesus is the ultimate revolution.

And a gentle revolution at that. Jesus returns to his tortured land, to the disciples who had scattered, not like Zeus or Mars fulminating in anger, not seeking revenge, but bearing the gift of peace. He exacts no retribution; there is no hell to pay. Neither does he unleash a riot of vengeance on the Temple or Rome. How unlike the gods of war. How unlike you and me, who can nurse grudges for decades.

None of that. No trace of condemnation. He had declared to Pilate that God's kingdom rejects violence.

Then he proved it on the cross and now again before his disciples. He forgives them, offers them even now his steadfast love. More, he banishes hierarchy. Lordliness bows to friendship: Jesus shows himself to be their friend.

On the shore of the Sea of Galilee, he makes them breakfast.

It's a touching, intimate scene. The disciples, having gone back to their livelihoods, pull into shore. Then we read: "When it was dawn, there on the shore stood Jesus." Waiting for them, looking forward to their return. The sentence is simple but brims with camaraderie and welcome. From the boat, with the sun rising, the disciples strain to make out his dark form in the distance. A beautiful new day, an image of peace, hope, and love. The risen Jesus stands silhouetted against a rising sun. He waits for them, and us.

A "charcoal fire" crackles nearby. And he invites them gently, "Come, have breakfast." They eat in silence, none daring "to ask who he was."

And here, I think, is the font of resurrection peace. Silence, a common meal, the risen Jesus present, the beauty of creation. I like to imagine the scene and place myself in the circle. There, in my prayerful imagining, I sense Jesus' peaceful presence and the soothing of my battered soul. In that intimate circle I feel new beginnings of love, hope, peace, even joy.

I urge you to try this. Conjure holy settings as you read them; let them be the context for forming your own peaceful life. From those spiritual settings, we too can go into the world of violence on a mission of liberation to lead humanity from its tombs.

It was certainly a new beginning for Simon Peter. As Jesus suffered torture, Peter disavowed any knowledge of him in front of the empire's "charcoal fire." Now he sits and eats before Christ's "charcoal fire."

He had denied knowing Jesus three times; now three times Jesus poses the question: "Simon Peter, do you love me?"

Three times: "Do you *agapao* me?"

And three times: "Yes, Lord. You know that I *phileo* you."

(*Phileo:* "brotherly love.")

Nonetheless, Jesus and Simon Peter are reconciled. And for the first time Jesus explicitly calls his impetuous friend to the life of nonviolence. "Simon Peter, follow me."

Jesus has risen, and he stands beyond all cultures of violence and war and above psychological urges toward rancor and ill will. In his gentle reunion he demonstrates nothing but *agape*, compassion, kindness, reconciliation, peace, and joy. And it transforms their hearts. We know this from the book of Acts. Upon Jesus' ascension, they take to the streets, form communities, confront injustice publicly, and offer their lives to embody Jesus' vision.

This is what the resurrection of Jesus has in store for us, as well. He calls us out of tombs of our own making and into the freedom of nonviolence. When we step into freedom we will, like the early community, have nothing to do with death anymore. We will not join the armed forces or fail to decry executions or make our livings in industries that design weapons. We will not make wealth our pursuit or hoard more than we need. We will not be violent to ourselves or to anyone. We will be nonviolent people offering the world compassion, *agape*, and peace.

Life is short, but our survival is guaranteed. So we can risk living in solidarity with all, especially the forsaken and even the enemies imposed on us by our nation. We can live life to the full, and so resist the forces of death, knowing that our resurrection has already begun.

This is the key to fullness of life here and now.

And it's a foretaste of eternity, at home in Jesus' circle, at peace with creation, our hearts healed in the aura of his love. This is our invitation to forsake the wiles of death and live life to the full.

Now we know it's true: *The kingdom of God is life.*

🖎

50

Our God of Love

Richard G. Malloy, SJ

"Your life is hidden with Christ in God."

Jesus and Satan were having an ongoing argument about who was better on the computer. They had been going at it for days, and God the Father was tired of hearing all of the bickering. Finally God said, "Cool it! I am going to set up a test that will run two hours and I will judge who does the better job."

So Satan and Jesus sat down at the keyboards and typed away. They worked Word. They excelled at Excel. They pounded out PowerPoint reports. They sent out e-mails with complicated attachments. They downloaded. They researched on the Web. They used Photoshop. But ten minutes before their time was up, lightning suddenly flashed across the sky, thunder clapped, the rain poured and, of course, the electricity went off.

Satan stared at his blank screen and screamed every curse word known in the underworld. Jesus just sighed. The electricity finally flickered back on and each of them restarted their computers. Satan started searching frantically and screamed, "It's gone! It's all gone! I lost everything when the power went off!"

Meanwhile, Jesus quietly started making pdf files of the past two hours of diligent work. Satan observed this and became irate. "Wait! He cheated! How did he do it?"

God shrugged and said, "Satan you of all fallen angels should know: Jesus saves."

Let me say something about (1) the truth that Jesus saves; (2) something about what the resurrection means, and (3) how we can believe it all.

Jesus saves us. From all sin. From all suffering. From all injustice. Wars and weapons, horrors and hate, torture and terror, fill the news. Teens commit suicide at alarming rates. Human trafficking ensnares young girls in 21st century forms of abject slavery. The never ending revelations of priest sex abuse and the charges of Bishops' covering up the sins/crimes goes on and on. All the bad news.

And then there's the personal tragedies and sadness of our days. A parent dies of cancer. Corporate malfeasance eliminates your job. A baseball player realizes he'll never make the majors. And on a much more mundane level, it's another year when I didn't lose twenty-five pounds during Lent!

Into all the bad news and failures of the world comes Jesus. Jesus saves! Jesus is risen! He is truly risen! Alleluia! We share in his resurrection. This is what we celebrate today. This is what we believe.

Easter Sunday a few years ago, the congregation was responding loudly and enthusiastically, "We do," to the renewal of our baptismal vows. As the last "We do" resounded through the church, a small, three-year-old girl, held in her father's arms, let out with a perfectly timed, "I don't." All present cracked up laughing. It was funny. But it raises the question, what do we believe about the resurrection? What does Jesus' resurrection mean for us?

Resurrection is not resuscitation or reanimation of a corpse. Resurrection is transformation. Resurrection is the promise of what will happen to those who die in Christ. Resurrection means "a complete transformation of the human being in his or her psychosomatic totality. Resurrection was thought of not as an event for the individual at death but as a corporate event. God would raise all the elect at the end of history."

The Son of God became what we are so we might become what God is. That's not some Jesuit spin on theology. That's St. Athanasius in the fourth century. Jesus' resurrection gives us the grace, i.e., the power, we need to be able to live with God forever.

Richard Dawkins and Christopher Hitchens, today's militant atheists, push their best-selling, but rather intellectually lightweight, polemical attacks on faith and religion. They say we are fools. Faith is ridiculous. Jesus died on the cross and that was it. Case closed. Death swallows us up in a meaningless, black void and we simply cease to exist.

Faith in the resurrection means we believe in life beyond this life, and that eternal life begins not when we die, but the moment we are baptized. We believe that the God who gives us existence, and preserves us alive all our days, will continue to give us the gift of life for all eternity. We know God has given us life now. Why would we assume God would stop giving us life when our bodies die? It seems to me that it makes more sense to hope for life beyond death. After all, I'm alive now, and that's quite a miracle.

Each of our cells holds some 20,000 different types of protein. That's some 100 million protein molecules in every one of our cells. There are some 20 million kilometers of DNA in the ten thousand trillion cells in our bodies. Your heart must pump 75 gallons of blood an hour, 1,800 gallons every day, 657,000 gallons a year.

Every one of the trillions of cells in our bodies will replace themselves several times during our earthly life. So even though our bodies change, we continue to exist. Why should we assume that the power that has made us will stop making us after our present body dies? It seems more reasonable a bet to think the God who has created us will continue to grace us with existence in a marvelously new, and hopefully thinner, resurrected body.

Life eternal is not like a change of horses where we ride off into a far distant sunset on another stallion. Karl Rahner, the great Jesuit theologian, taught that the resurrection means we become all we could ever have been. All the limits of this life are lifted and we are all we could ever hope and desire to be.

According to Jesuit David Stanley, the resurrection

means that the Kingdom of God has arrived on this earth. New Testament authors intimate that heaven means we join Jesus in his reign over the "course of world history. Heaven . . . is not a kind of perennial 'Old Folks Home.' It is not simply a place of retirement and celestial repose for senior citizens of the kingdom of God. Heaven consists in the active participation in the glorified Christ's direction of history."

Last year, a man who was literally a second father to me died after a long bout with prostate cancer. Big Leo had withered away to a point where his adult children and I were taking turns providing hospice care to him. A few weeks later, a fishing buddy, Charlie, died. Another cancer victim.

I've been given the gift of faith. I believe I will see Leo and Charlie again. I believe we all will be transformed in Christ to live together in a "kingdom of truth and life, a kingdom of holiness and grace, a kingdom of justice love and peace" (Preface, Feast of Christ the King).

All of us have lost loved ones. Where are they? How are they? Rahner writes: "The great mistake of many people . . . is to imagine that those whom death has taken, leave us. They do not leave us. They remain! Where are they? In the darkness? Oh, no. It is we who are in darkness. We do not see them, but they see us. Their eyes radiant with glory, are fixed upon our eyes. . . . Though invisible to us, our dead are not absent. . . . They are living near us transfigured into light and power and love."

How can we believe this good news, this wonderful revelation of our God of love? Pray. Prayer reveals reality to us. Thomas Merton wrote, "Prayer is a real source of personal freedom in the midst of a world in which men are dominated by massive organizations and rigid institutions which seek only to exploit them for money and power. Far from being a source of alienation true religion in spirit is a liberating force that helps man to find himself in God."

Let's find ourselves in God, this God who loves us, this God who saves us. Let us pray.

🌿

51

Seven Stanzas at Easter

John Updike

Make no mistake: if he rose at all
It was as His body;
If the cell's dissolution did not reverse, the
    molecule reknit,
The amino acids rekindle,
The Church will fall.

It was not as the flowers,
Each soft spring recurrent;
It was not as His Spirit in the mouths and
    fuddled eyes of the
Eleven apostles;
It was as His flesh; ours.

The same hinged thumbs and toes
The same valved heart
That-pierced-died, withered, paused, and then
    regathered
Out of enduring Might
New strength to enclose.

Let us not mock God with metaphor,
Analogy, sidestepping, transcendence,
Making of the event a parable, a sign painted in
    the faded
Credulity of earlier ages:
Let us walk through the door.

The stone is rolled back, not papier-mache,
Not a stone in a story,
But the vast rock of materiality that in the slow
    grinding of
Time will eclipse for each of us
The wide light of day.

And if we have an angel at the tomb,
Make it a real angel,
Weighty with Max Planck's quanta, vivid with
    hair, opaque in

All Shall Be Well

The dawn light, robed in real linen
Spun on a definite loom.

Let us not seek to make it less monstrous,
For our own convenience, our own sense of
      beauty,
Lest, awakened in one unthinkable hour, we are
      embarrassed
By the miracle,
And crushed by remonstrance.

🖎

52

Always and Forever, the Final Word

Richard Rohr, OFM

"Think of what is above, not of what is on Earth."

Don't you often wonder why so much of human life seems so futile, so tragic, so short, or so sad? If Christ has risen, and we speak so much of being risen with Christ, then why do most people experience their life as tragic more than triumphant? Why is there non-stop war? Why are there so many people unjustly imprisoned? Why are the poor oppressed? Why, even in Christian nations, is there a long history of deceit and injustice? Why do so few marriages last, even among those of us who say that we believe? Why are there so many children born with disabilities? Why do we destroy so many of our relationships? Why?

What are you up to, God? Why is there so much suffering if Christ has risen? It really doesn't make any logical sense. Is the Resurrection something that just happened once in Jesus's body, but not in ours? Or not in human history? When and where and how is this resurrection thing really happening? Is it only after death? Is it only in the next world? My guess is that it is both now and later, and *just enough now* to promise you an also infinite forever.

The Resurrection of Christ is telling us that in the Great Story Line of History, in the mind of God as it were, the Final Judgment has already happened, and it's nothing that we need to be afraid of. Instead, the arc of history is moving toward resurrection. God's Final Judgment is that God will have the last word, that there are no dead-ends, that our lives and human history is not going to end in a sad and tragic list of human crucifixions and natural disasters. When we look at life in its daily moments, this is almost always hard to see. We can only see in small frames. Yet over and over again, here and there, more than we suspect, a kind of cosmic hope breaks through for those who are willing to see and willing to cooperate with this universal mystery of Resurrection. I am never sure if the promise of resurrection creates an intuitive hope in us, or if people who grasp onto hope can also believe in resurrection. All I know is that both are the work of the Holy Spirit within us.

In this part of the world, Easter coincides with Spring-time. I hope that you're noticing the leaves and the flowers being reborn after months of winter. I went out this April morning to watch the sunrise which I was told would rise at 6:30 a.m. But on the west side of the Sandia Mountain Range where I live, it takes a little longer for the sun to make an appearance. I found myself waiting, and waiting. But sure enough, at the very moment of 7:00 a.m., the sun again, as it always inevitably does, peeked over the mountains.

I thought, "You know, this is not so much like a sunrise as a groundswell coming from the earth." It was coming from the world in which you and I live. It was coming, not from the top, but from the bottom. It was saying, "Even all of this which looks muddy and material, even all of this which looks so ordinary and dying will be reborn." Sunrises and springtime cannot be stopped, even when winter holds us with its desperate grip. Maybe this is why ancient people almost worshiped the seasons, and why they themselves became spiritual teachers.

This is the Feast Day of Hope. As the poet e.e. cummings puts it, "I who have died am alive again today, and this is the sun's birthday; this is the birth day of life and love and wings: and of the gay great happening illimitably earth." Jesus is the stand-in for everybody. He gives history a personal, a historical, and a cosmic hope. His one life tells us where it is all heading. He is the microcosm of the whole divine and human cosmos!

This is the feast that says God will have the last word and that whatever we crucify, whatever we tragically destroy, God will undo with his eternal love and forgiveness. This feast affirms that God's Final Judgment is Resurrection, that God will turn all that remains, all the destruction and hurt and punishment, into beauty. The word on that usually blank white banner that we see the Risen Christ carrying in Christian art is simple and clear: LOVE IS STRONGER THAN DEATH! God's love will always win! That's what it means to be God.

Without such hope why would you keep living and believing when you see that everything passes on and passes away? Everything is here and gone, here and gone, here and gone. If you haven't noticed that yet, just wait a while. Everything passes. This becomes overwhelming for most people as they get older, and it is often just denied because it is so painful. Without such cosmic hope, we all become cynics. Yet the Christian promise is that God will replace everything with his immeasurable and infinite life. Jesus is the standing promise that this is the case.

What the Resurrection is saying, more than anything else, is that love is stronger than death. Jesus walked through both life and death with love, which becomes an infinite life, a participation in God himself. Surprise of surprises! This cannot be proven logically or rationally, and yet this is the mystery that we now stake our life—and our death—on: *nothing dies forever, and all that has died in love will be reborn in an even larger love.*

So, to be a Christian, brothers and sisters, is to be inevitably and forever a person of hope. You cannot stay in your depression. You cannot stay in your darkness because it's only for a time. No feeling is final. It will not last. God in Christ is saying, "This is what will last—my life and my love will always and forever have the final word."

❦

53

Jesus and His Wounds

Robert Schreiter, CPPS

The risen Jesus is a survivor. He has been through abuse and torture. He has been beaten, mocked, and had thorns pressed into his head. He has experienced public humiliation and been executed on the cross. He has experienced the pit of death. And now he has been raised from the dead.

We cannot get inside Jesus' own experience of this. Piero della Francesca's painting of Jesus risen tries to capture what might have been part of that experience. Jesus looks a little dazed or bewildered, as though this will take some getting used to. The experience of resurrection life has nothing with which it can be compared. It is not the same as resuscitation from death, as Lazarus experienced, for those who have been so resuscitated die once again. In the appearance stories, Jesus' body is indeed glorified, but the scars of his torture remain. His body has both discontinuity and continuity with his past.

It is interesting to see how Jesus deals with his wounds. In Luke's account of the appearance in the upper room, Jesus volunteers to show the disciples his wounds. It is as though he is a little amazed about them himself. These are wounds that do not go away, but link Jesus forever to his passion and death. In this, Jesus is like every survivor who must bear the burden of those wounds for the rest of his or her life. Jesus shows the disciples his wounds and talks about them freely, because they are no longer a source of pain and painful memory, but now, in the case of Thomas, become wounds that heal. They heal Thomas's troubled soul, riddled with the loss of faith and hope. Jesus' wounds have a remarkable quality, therefore. They link him back to his own death, but point ahead to life and hope as well.

But how do wounds heal? How do they make someone else whole? Wounds, first of all, mark a break in the surface of things. A smooth surface does not prompt reflection or thought. It takes the disruption of that smooth surface to give us pause to ponder.

Wounds are an invitation to become aware of how fragile the human body is, how easily it is penetrated. They remind us that all our arrangements, personal and social, can be easily disrupted. The violence that wounds do to the tissues of a body—cutting through the delicate layers, disrupting the functions—puts into question how much we can rely upon things to be as they should be. Wounds are question marks about existence.

An open wound allows us to peer inside the body, below the surface of things, and to discover there that what is underneath is not like what first appears to the eye. We see structures and processes that support the surface but look very different in themselves. We become aware that so much of our world is not what it seems. To reach this realization may undermine trust for some. That wounds can occur, that they can be deliberately inflicted, makes the world a very unsafe place. For others, it is an invitation to contemplate the complexity of the world and how much human flourishing relies on a capacity to trust. Trust itself is as fragile as those broken surfaces we contemplate, yet without trust there is no full human life.

Vulnerability—literally, the ability to be wounded —is a kind of self-giving in love that makes possible coming to a new place, a new state of existence. Vulnerability is not about masochism, or a desire to draw attention to oneself or to be pitied. Vulnerability is a capacity so to trust that one runs the risk of wounds. It does not make wounds desirable, nor does it make them less painful. One is willing to run the risk of wounds because of something more important: the communion of love that engenders trust, that makes the fresh start of forgiveness possible.

When Thomas is invited to touch Jesus' wounds, those wounds draw out of him the disruptions below the surface of his own life. His trust has been shaken, his faith in Jesus as the messenger of God's reign has been called into question. Touching the wounds of Jesus connects his inner wounds to those very visible ones of Jesus. The wounds of Thomas's heart can be placed in the larger and deeper wounds of Jesus, hands and side. In this way, Thomas is healed and can move from doubt to his confession of faith.

Wounds have knowledge. Those who have suffered physical wounds that have changed their bodies know how a change in weather can signal itself in their old wounds. Onsets of tension or stress sometimes register in the same way. And wounds may also be the point where the decline of age announces itself. When those wounds are touched, or when environmental changes make them ache, the memories of their infliction instantly come back. Wounds bear, therefore, a kind of knowledge. They become repositories of memories of traumas that are now past, but whose infliction has forever altered a life.

It is the knowledge wounds hear that gives them a healing quality for others. When Thomas touched the wounds of Jesus' crucifixion, it was as though the memories in those wounds provided a way of reorganizing Thomas's own experience. His memories were no longer troubling to him, because they had been transfigured into a confession of who Jesus had become. Wounds can heal because, having the memory of trauma, they can connect to the wounds of others. They know the experience of disruption and pain. The transfigured wounds of Jesus have not lost that quality of memory. The transfiguring wounds of Jesus' crucifixion hold that memory in a special way. It is a memory that cannot be erased; it will always be part of him.

But it is only such memory that can touch the trauma of memory in another.

People are usually afraid to touch wounds, either for fear of hurting the wounded person or for fear of contagion. Jesus, however, invites others to touch his wounds. His wounds have become redemptive. They heal others; they are contagious through the spread, not of disease, but of the alleviation of suffering. The wounds of those who have experienced the trauma of war or of torture are not worn as badges of honor, although others on occasion may treat them that way. They more likely still ache than glow. But those wounds give the reconciled the possibility of entry into the wounds of others. They become healing wounds, wounds that render the wounds of others less painful. Their wounds know about healing—how long it takes, how incomplete the healing will always be. It is the knowledge of the patience needed, and the realization that wounds can always produce new pain that make the wounds of the reconciled so sensitive to the wounds of others. It is little wonder, then, that it is the reconciled who are our best leaders in any process of reconciliation.

54

That Nature Is a Heraclitean Fire and of the Comfort of the Resurrection

Gerard Manley Hopkins

CLOUD-PUFFBALL, torn tufts, tossed pillows
' flaunt forth, then chevy on an air-
built thoroughfare: heaven-roysterers, in gay-
gangs ' they throng; they glitter in marches.
Down roughcast, down dazzling whitewash, '
wherever an elm arches,
Shivelights and shadowtackle in long ' lashes
lace, lance, and pair.
Delightfully the bright wind boisterous ' ropes,
wrestles, beats earth bare
Of yestertempest's creases; in pool and rut peel
parches

Squandering ooze to squeezed ' dough, crust,
     dust; stanches, starches
Squadroned masks and manmarks ' treadmire
     toil there
Footfretted in it. Million-fuelèd, ' nature's bon-
     fire burns on.
But quench her bonniest, dearest ' to her, her
     clearest-selvèd spark
Man, how fast his firedint, ' his mark on mind,
     is gone!
Both are in an unfathomable, all is in an enor-
     mous dark
Drowned. O pity and indig ' nation! Manshape,
     that shone
Sheer off, disseveral, a star, ' death blots black
     out; nor mark
        Is any of him at all so stark
But vastness blurs and time ' beats level.
        Enough! the Resurrection,
A heart's-clarion! Away grief's gasping, ' joyless
     days, dejection.
        Across my foundering deck shone
A beacon, an eternal beam. ' Flesh fade, and
     mortal trash
Fall to the residuary worm; ' world's wildfire,

leave but ash:
>   In a flash, at a trumpet crash,
I am all at once what Christ is, ' since he was
>   what I am, and
This Jack, joke, poor potsherd, ' patch, match-
>   wood, immortal diamond,
>   Is immortal diamond.

Sources and Acknowledgments

Orbis Books has made every effort to identify the owner of each selection in this book, and to obtain permission from the author, publisher, or agent in question. In the event of inadvertent errors, please notify us so that we can correct the next printing.

1. T. S. Eliot, excerpt from "Ash Wednesday," from *Collected Poems 1909–1962*, by T. S. Eliot. Copyright © 1936 by Houghton Mifflin Harcourt Publishing Company. Copyright © renewed 1964 by Thomas Stearns Eliot. Reprinted by permission of Houghton Mifflin Harcourt Publishing Company. All rights reserved.

2. Thomas Merton, "Spiritual Medicine," originally titled "Ash Wednesday" from *Seasons of Celebration* by Thomas Merton. Copyright © 1965 by The Abbey of Gethsemani. Copyright renewed 1993 by Robert Giroux, James Laughlin and Tommy O'Callaghan. Reprinted by permission of Farrar, Straus and Giroux, LLC.

3. Joan Chittister, OSB, "A Time to Heal," from *For Everything a Season*. Orbis Books, 1995, 2013.

4. Paul Brandeis Raushenbush, "Why I Love Lent," *The Blog*, March 10, 2014, www.huffingtonpost.com. Used by permission of the author.

5. Mallory McDuff, "Why I'm Committed to Lent," April 1, 2014, www.huffingtonpost.com. Used by permission of the author.

6. James Martin, SJ, "Bothering to Love: One Priest's Modest Proposal for Lent," April 28, 2010, www.huffingtonpost.com. Used by permission of the author.

7. Christopher Frechette, "Lenten Observance Transforms Us from Cacophony to Symphony," *National Catholic Reporter*, March 2014. Used by permission of the author.

8. Carlo Carretto, "Under the Great Rock," from *Letters from the Desert*, Orbis Books, 2002.

9. Ita Ford, MM, "I Hope You Find," Letter to Jennifer Sullivan, dated August 16, 1980, reprinted from *"Here I Am, Lord:" The Letters and Writings of Ita Ford*, Orbis Books, 2005.

10. Rob Bell, "A God Who Provides," from *Sick, and You Cared for Me*, ed. Deacon Jim Knipper, Clear Faith Publishing, 2014. Reprinted by permission of the author.

11. Pope John XXIII, "Prayer for the Beginning of Lent," broadcast February 28, 1963, and reprinted in *Journal of a Soul: The Autobiography of Pope John XXIII*. Copyright © 1965, 1980 by Geoffrey Chapman, a division of Cassell Ltd. Reprinted by permission of Bloomsbury Publishing Plc.

12. Ted Loder, "Catch Me in My Scurrying," from *Guerrillas of Grace* by Ted Loder. Copyright © 1984, 2005 by Ted Loder, admin. Augsburg Fortress. Reproduced by permission of Augsburg Fortress.

13. Mother Mary Joseph Rogers, MM, "Not Servants, But Friends," excerpts from Mother Mary Joseph's Sunday Conference, February 27, 1938, Maryknoll, NY.

14. Ernesto Cardenal, "The Temptations in the Wilderness," from *The Gospel in Solentiname*, Orbis Books, 2010.

15. Phyllis Tickle, "Final Sanity," from *Wisdom in the Waiting: Spring's Sacred Days*. Copyright © 1987 by Phyllis A. Tickle; First Loyola Press printing, 2004. "Final Sanity," has appeared in a number of publications, including *The Tennessee Churchman*, for which it won the Polly Bond Award in 1985. Reprinted by permission of the author.

16. Kerry Weber, "A Complicated Grief," originally published in *America* magazine on September 22, 2014. Used by permission of the author.

17. Dorothy Day, "A Lifetime Job," from *Dorothy Day: Selected Writings*, Orbis Books, 2005.

18. Joe Hoover, "Flaw," *The Jesuit Post*, April 4, 2012, www.jesuitpost.org. Used by permission of the author.

19. Donald McQuade, MM, "A Sign of Life," unpublished reflection. Used by permission of the author.

20. Hob Osterlund, "Bald Places," published in the *Portland Magazine*, Winter 2007. Used by permission of the author.

21. Pope Francis, "Message for Lent," Message of His Holiness Pope Francis for Lent 2015, October 4, 2014. Copyright © Libreria Editrice Vaticana. Used by permission of Libreria Editrice Vaticana.

22. Peter Quinn, "Things Fall Apart," *Commonweal*, March 25, 2015. Copyright © 2015 by *Commonweal*. Used with permission.

23. James T. Keane, "A Rose by Any Other Name," *The Jesuit Post*, February 12, 2012, www.jesuitpost.org. Used by permission of the author.

24. Joyce Rupp, "Eastering Joy," original reflection. Used by permission of the author.

25. Jim Forest, "Two Old People and a Young Man with a Gun," reprinted from *Loving Our Enemies*, Orbis Books, 2014.

26. Paul Myers, "The River," published in the *Portland Magazine*, Summer 2008. Used by permission of the author.

27. Leonardo Boff, "It Is in Pardoning that We Are Pardoned," reprinted from *The Prayer of Saint Francis*, Orbis Books, 2012.

28. Mary Oliver, "Spring," from *West Wind: Poems and Prose Poems* by Mary Oliver. Copyright © 1997 by Mary Oliver. Reprinted by permission of Houghton Mifflin Harcourt Publishing Company. All rights reserved.

29. Matt Malone, SJ, "The Father of Mercies," originally published in *America* on March 7, 2005. Used by permission of the author.

30. Jean Vanier, "Reading the Gospels," from *Our Life Together* by Jean Vanier. Copyright © 2007 by Jean Vanier. HarperCollins Publishers Ltd., 2007. Used with permission. All rights reserved.

31. Howard Thurman, "Near Journey's End," from *Deep Is the Hunger*, Friends United Press, 1978. Used by permission of Friends United Meeting.

32. Daniel Berrigan, SJ, "The Face of Christ," from *Testimony: The Word Made Fresh*, Orbis Books, 2004.

33. Caryll Houselander, "Transfigured," from *The Risen Christ: Forty Days after the Resurrection*, Scepter Publishers, 2007. Used with permission.

34. Malcolm Boyd, "Be Kind to Prophets." Used by permission of the Estate of Malcolm Boyd.

35. Julia Alvarez, "Fifteen Stations in the Passion According to Mark." Copyright © 2014 by Julia Alvarez. Used by permission of Stuart Bernstein Representation for Artists, New York, NY, and protected by the Copyright Laws of the United States. All rights reserved. The printing, copying, redistribution, or retransmission of this content without express permission is prohibited.

36. Virgil Elizondo, "Way of the Cross," from *Way of the Cross: The Passion of Christ in the Americas*, Orbis Books, 1992.

37. Greg Boyle, SJ, "Following in Footsteps," from *Sick, and You Cared for Me*, Deacon Jim Knipper, ed., Clear Faith Publishing, 2014. Reprinted by permission of the author.

38. Sheila Cassidy, "Foot-washing of a Different Sort," from *Sharing the Darkness*, Orbis Books, 1992.

39. Michael Leach, "Good Friday and Easter Sunday Are One," *National Catholic Reporter*, March 27, 2012.

40. Greg Kandra, "Good Friday: I Am Here," from *Hungry, and You Fed Me*, Deacon Jim Knipper, ed., Clear Faith Publishing, 2012. Used by permission of the author.

41. William J. Bausch, "God Is a Loving Aunt," from *Once Upon a Gospel: Inspiring Homilies and Insightful Reflections* by William J. Bausch. Copyright © 2008. Twenty-Third Publications.

42. Mary Lou Kownacki, "It Is Finished in Beauty," from *A Monk in the Inner City*, Orbis Books, 2008.

43. Henri Nouwen, "Jesus Falls for the Third Time," from *Walk with Jesus: Stations of the Cross*, Orbis Books, 1990, 2015. Copyright © 1990 by the Henri Nouwen Legacy Trust.

44. Brian Doyle, "Did the Jesus Man Die?," from *The Thorny Grace of It and Other Essays for Imperfect Catholics*, Loyola Press, 2013. Copyright 2013 by Brian Doyle. Used by permission of the author.

45. Mary Christine Athans, "Crucifixion and Resurrection" from *In Quest of the Jewish Mary*, Orbis Books, 2013.

46. Howard Thurman, "The Glad Surprise," from *Meditations of the Heart* by Howard Thurman. Copyright © 1953, 1981 by Anne Thurman. Reprinted by permission of Beacon Press, Boston.

47. Edwina Gateley, "Tell Them," from *A Warm Moist Salty God: Women Journeying Towards Wisdom*, Source Books, September 1993. Used by permission of the author.

48. William O'Malley, SJ, "Very Early Sunday Morning," from *The Week that Opened Forever*, Orbis Books, 2014.

49. John Dear, "The Resurrection of the Nonviolent Jesus," from *Lazarus, Come Forth!*, Orbis Books, 2011.

50. Richard G. Malloy, SJ, "Our God of Love," from *Hungry, and You Fed Me*, Deacon Jim Knipper, ed., Clear Faith Publishing, 2012. Reprinted by permission of the author.

51. John Updike, "Seven Stanzas at Easter," from *Telephone Poles and Other Poems* by John Updike. Copyright © 1958, 1959, 1960, 1961, 1962, 1963 by John Updike. Used by permission of Alfred A. Knopf, an imprint of the Knopf Doubleday Publishing Group, a division of Penguin Random House LLC. All rights reserved.

52. Richard Rohr, OFM, "Always and Forever, the Final Word," from *Sick, and You Cared for Me*, Deacon Jim Knipper, ed., Clear Faith Publishing, 2014. Reprinted by permission of the author.

53. Robert Schreiter, CPPS, "Jesus and His Wounds," from *The Ministry of Reconciliation*, Orbis Books, 1998.

54. Gerard Manley Hopkins, "That Nature Is a Heraclitean Fire and of the Comfort of the Resurrection," from *Poems*. London: Humphrey Milford, 1918.

Index of Contributors

Julia Alvarez is a Dominican-American novelist, poet and essayist. Notable works include *How The García Girls Lost Their Accents* and *In the Time of the Butterflies*. **35**

Mary Christine Athans, BVM, is a Sister of Charity of the Blessed Virgin Mary and the author of *In Quest of The Jewish Mary*. She is professor emerita at the Saint Paul Seminary School of Divinity of the University of St. Thomas (Minnesota). **45**

William J. Bausch, a priest of the Diocese of Trenton, New Jersey, is author of numerous books, including the bestsellers *The Yellow Brick Road* and *A New Look at the Sacrament*. **41**

Rob Bell is a bestselling author, international teacher, and highly sought after public speaker. His books include *Love Wins, What We Talk about When We Talk about God, Jesus Wants to Save Christians*, and *Drops Like Stars*. In 2011 he was profiled in *Time* as one of the one hundred most influential people in the world. **10**

Daniel Berrigan, SJ, is a Jesuit priest, poet, and longtime activist for peace and social justice. Among his many books are *Testimony; Ezekiel; Uncommon Prayer*; and (with Thich Nhat Hanh) *The Raft Is Not the Shore* **32**

Leonardo Boff is a Brazilian theologian considered to be one of the founders of liberation theology. He has written more than eighty books, including *Jesus Christ Liberator; Christianity in a Nutshell; Francis of Rome, Francis of Assisi; and Come Holy Spirit: Inner Fire, Giver of Life and Comforter of the Poor*. **27**

Malcolm Boyd (d. 2015) became an Episcopal priest in 1955 after a successful career in advertising and television, and served parishes and college chaplaincies in Indianapolis, Colorado, Detroit, Washington DC, and Santa Monica. *Time Magazine* dubbed him "the

Index of Contributors

John Dear is a priest, peace activist, organizer, lecturer, and retreat leader, and the author/editor of more than twenty books on peace and nonviolence, including *Thomas Merton, Peacemaker* **49**

Brian Doyle is editor of *Portland Magazine* and author of many books of essays and fiction, notably the novels *Mink River* and *The Plover*, and most recently *How the Light Gets In & Other Headlong Epiphanies*, a book of proems published in 2015. His work has appeared in *The Atlantic Monthly*, *Harper's*, *The New York Times*, and in many other periodicals around the world. **44**

T. S. Eliot (d. 1965) was the acclaimed author of "The Waste Land," "Four Quartets," and "The Love Song of J. Alfred Prufrock," among numerous other poems, prose, and works of drama. He won the Nobel Prize for Literature in 1948. . . . . **1**

Virgil Elizondo is a theologian, author, pastor, and popular speaker nationwide. A former rector of San Fernando Cathedral, he is director of Archdiocesan Television Ministry for San Antonio, Texas. Among his books are *God of Surprises* and *Galilean Journey* . . . **36**

Ita Ford, MM (d. 1980), was a Maryknoll missionary in Bolivia, Chile, and El Salvador. She worked with the poor and war refugees. On December 2, 1980, she was murdered in El Salvador along with fellow missionaries Sister Maura Clarke, MM; Jean Donovan; and Dorothy Kazel, OSU, by a death squad of the right-wing Salvadoran military-led government **9**

Jim Forest is a writer, theologian, educator, and peace activist. His many books include *All Is Grace: A Biography of Dorothy Day*; *Living with Wisdom: A Life of Thomas Merton*; and *Loving Our Enemies: Reflections on the Hardest Commandment* **25**

Pope Francis, the former archbishop of Buenos Aires, was elected pope on March 13, 2013. . . . . **21**

Christopher Frechette is a biblical scholar teaching at St. Mary's University, San Antonio, TX. **7**

All Shall Be Well

Edwina Gateley is founder of the Volunteer Missionary Movement and Genesis House, as well as an internationally recognized minister, conference speaker, poet, and spiritual writer **47**

Joe Hoover, SJ, is a Jesuit brother and the poetry editor at *America* magazine. A New York writer and actor, he also works at St. Ignatius Grammar School **18**

Gerard Manley Hopkins, SJ (d. 1889), was a Jesuit priest widely considered one of the greatest poets of the Victorian Era **54**

Caryll Houselander (d. 1954) was an English mystic, ecclesiastical artist, poet, and author. Her 1944 book of essays about Mary, *The Reed of God*, established her as a popular modern Catholic spiritual writer **33**

Pope John XXIII (d. 1963) reigned from 1958 until his death in 1963 and convened Vatican II. Known as "Good Pope John," he was canonized by Pope Francis in 2014 . . . . **11**

Greg Kandra is a Roman Catholic deacon serving the Diocese of Brooklyn, New York. He worked for twenty-six years as a writer and producer for CBS News in both New York and Washington. He is the creator of "The Deacon's Bench" blog and is the multimedia editor for the Catholic Near East Welfare Association. **40**

James T. Keane is an editor at Orbis Books and a columnist for *America* magazine.. . . . . **23**

Mary Lou Kownacki, OSB, is a Benedictine sister of Erie, PA. She is the author of *A Monk in the Inner City: The ABCs of a Spiritual Journey* and editor of *Joan Chittister: The Essential Writings* **42**

Michael Leach is publisher emeritus and editor-at-large of Orbis Books. A leader in Catholic publishing for thirty years, he has edited and published more than two thousand books. In 2007, the Catholic Book Publishers Association honored him with a Lifetime Achievement Award. Dubbed "the dean of Catholic book publishing" by *U.S. Catholic* magazine, he has also authored or edited the

Index of Contributors

bestsellers *I Like Being Catholic, A Maryknoll Book of Prayer, The People's Catechism, Goodness and Light,* and *I Like Being Married.* **39**

Ted Loder is a retired United Methodist minister who served as senior pastor for thirty-eight years at Philadelphia's First United Methodist Church of Germantown, well known for its dynamic worship and preaching as well as its urban involvement and prophetic social action. He has published several books of prayers, sermons, and commentary including *Guerrillas of Grace* and *Loaves, Fishes and Leftovers* **12**

Richard G. Malloy, SJ, is a Jesuit priest and Vice President for University Ministries at the University of Scranton. He is the author of the books *A Faith That Frees* and *Being on Fire: The Top Ten Essentials of Catholic Faith* **50**

Matt Malone, SJ, is a Jesuit priest and the Editor-in-Chief of *America* magazine **29**

James Martin, SJ, is a Jesuit priest, an editor at *America* magazine, and a well-known American spiritual writer. He is a frequent media commentator and was the "official chaplain" of *The Colbert Report.* **6**

Mallory McDuff teaches environmental education at Warren Wilson College in the Swannanoa Valley near Asheville, NC. She is author of *Sacred Acts: How Churches Are Working to Save Earth's Climate.* She has a Ph.D. in wildlife ecology and conservation, with a focus on environmental education...........................**5**

Donald McQuade, MM, is a Maryknoll priest who served for more than forty years in the Philippines, where his ministries included clinical pastoral education, counseling alcoholics and drug addicts, retreat work, parish apostolates, and writing **19**

Thomas Merton (d. 1968) was a Trappist monk, author of over sixty books on topics ranging from civil rights to nuclear arms to monastic life, and one of the most influential American spiritual writers of the twentieth century. **2**

ALL SHALL BE WELL

Index of Contributors

Joyce Rupp is the author of numerous bestselling books, including *Open the Door* and *Fragments of Your Ancient Name*. She is a member of the Servite (Servants of Mary) community and the co-director of the Institute of Compassionate Presence **24**

Robert Schreiter, CPPS, is a priest of the Missionaries of the Precious Blood. He has published seventeen books in the areas of inculturation, world mission, and reconciliation. Among them are *Constructing Local Theologies; The New Catholicity: Theology between the Global and the Local; Reconciliation: Mission and Ministry in a Changing Social Order*; and *The Ministry of Reconciliation: Spirituality and Strategies*. He is past president of both the American Society of Missiology and the Catholic Theological Society of America.. **53**

Howard Thurman (d. 1981) was an influential African American author, philosopher, theologian, and civil rights leader. He was Dean of Chapel at Howard University and Boston University for more than two decades, wrote twenty-one books, and is considered one of the greatest African-American preachers of the early twentieth century **31, 46**

Phyllis Tickle is the author of over three dozen books on religion and spirituality and a prominent lecturer on religion in America. She is the founding editor of the Religion Department of *Publishers Weekly*. **15**

John Updike (d. 2009) was a renowned American novelist, poet, short story writer, art critic, and literary critic **51**

Jean Vanier is a philosopher, theologian, and author of more than thirty books. He is the founder of L'Arche, an international network of communities where people with and without intellectual disabilities live and work together in faith and friendship. In 2015, he was awarded the Templeton Prize for his "innovative discovery of the central role of vulnerable people in the creation of a more just, inclusive and humane society." **30**

Kerry Weber is the managing editor of *America* magazine and the author of the award-winning book *Mercy in the City*. **16**